D1189568

BOARD GAMES
GAMES
~THAT TELL~
STORIES

IGNACY TRZEWICZEK

IGNACY TRZEWICZEK

Hello!

Ttrewela
2015

Portal Games

Ignacy Trzewiczek

Ignacy
Trzewiczek

IGNACY
TRZEWICZEK

IGNACY TRZEWICZEK

Ignacy
Trzewiczek

IGNACY
TRZEWICZEK

IGNACY
TRZEWICZEK

IGNACY TRZEWICZEK

Ignacy was born on September 23, 1976. Married to Merry and a father of two, he lives in Bojszów, a village near Gliwice, Poland. In 1999 he founded the RPG magazine 'Portal' and a company to publish it, becoming a publisher and soon after a designer.

Follow me on twitter: @trzewik
Follow me on instagram: @trzewik
Subscribe to: http://boardgamesthattellstories.com
Follow me on facebook: https://www.facebook.com/trzewiczek

IGNACY'S DESIGNS AND CO-DESIGNS

Role Playing Games
Władca Zimy (2001), an unofficial supplement for Warhammer Fantasy Roleplay

Neuroshima RPG (2002) and its supplements (2003-2010), a postapocalyptic RPG

Monastyr (2004) and its supplements (2004-2010), a dark fantasy RPG

Play Smart (2010), *Play Tricky* (2011) - RPG Game Master's almanacs

Board Games
Machina (The Machine) (2002)
Gody (Courtship) (2003)
Zombiaki (Zombies) (2003)
Machina 2: Reloaded (2006)
Władcy Smoków (Dragon Lords) (2007)
Witchcraft (2008)
Stronghold (2009)
Prêt-à-Porter (2010)
51st State (2010)
Stronghold: Undead (2010)
Zombiaki 2: Attack on Moscow (2010)
New Era (2011)
Winter (2012)
Convoy (2012)
Robinson Crusoe: Adventure on the Cursed Island (2012)
Voyage of the Beagle (2013)
Imperial Settlers (2014)
Why Can't We Be Friends (2014)
The Witcher Adventure Game (2014)
Ruins (2014)
Five Families (2015)
Stronghold 2nd ed (2015)
Atlanteans (2015)
Rattle, Battle, Grab the Loot (2015)

THANKS!

I'd like to thank all designers who agreed to contribute to the book, I'd like to thank all fans who made this book possible and backed the project, I'd like to thank all people who play my games and let me do what I love and I'd like to thank Merry for everything. Thank you!

Thank you!

BOARD GAMES ~THAT TELL~ STORIES

2

IGNACY TRZEWICZEK

Imperial Settlers cards, one of first prototypes.

CONSPIRACY THEORY

At least once a month I receive an email from a paranoid game designer. He wants to submit a game to Portal Games, but before he does that, he asks me how I can assure him that I won't steal his idea.

We all know that that is exactly what I do, right? I sit at my desk and I wait for a new prototype. I check my inbox every hour to see if a new idea has been submitted, a great game that I can steal, publish as my own design, and win Spiel des Jahres.

That is exactly what I do and that's exactly who I am. The hunter in the dark. A predator looking for easy prey, young designers. Yeah…

***

First things first. If you think that I am a thief, if you think that I want to steal your idea, if you think that I am a jerk… Why would you contact me in the first place? Why would you even bother?

Do you think I steal ideas? Don't contact me. It is as simple as that.

Then. Think. A little. Please.

If I steal your idea and publish it as my own design, what would you do? You'd go to BGG, you'd write that it was your idea first. You'd show scans of your prototype. You'd ask your friends who tested your prototype to confirm that they played this prototype with you.

That is the moment I am screwed for good.

Never will an author submit his game to me again.

Portal Games steals game ideas.

I am dead in the water, out of business in 3 months. No one will buy my games anymore.

Even the best prototype is not worth stealing. Trust me.

***

Don't be paranoid. No one wants to rob you. No one has any interest in stealing your ideas. Let's face it, the royalties for designers are not that big anyway.

Send your prototypes to publishers without fear. The worst thing that could happen would be the publisher refusing to publish your game. The best that could happen? A great adventure with your own game published and then praised by players all around the world. Interested?

GIVE THEM A SECOND CHANCE

I played *Android: Netrunner*. The first game was terrible. I had problems with the rules because the rulebook is terrible. I played, but there weren't too many choices to be made. You play an Agenda, then place an Ice in front of it, and wait for the Runner to attack. Boring. Meh.

I spent some more time with the rulebook. I went through the BGG forums. I asked my employee Lukas to help me with the rules because still some things were unclear to me. We played again. It didn't rock. It was quite boring, in fact. Play an Agenda, put Ice out in front of it, gather money, wait.

I visited BGG again. The game has extremely good ratings. Everybody is just crazy about the game. We played it again. Well, it was okay. I lost, but I wanted a rematch.

We played again. It was quite fun. For a few rounds it was really exciting. I lost. I wanted a rematch. We played again. It was fun. It was exciting. I lost again...

***

These days the pressure of new titles waiting on your shelf is huge. You play the game. Either it is great or it sucks. No middle ground.

No time for a second chance. No time for games that are just okay. There are 10 new releases waiting on your shelf. You have no time to give a game another chance, right? Either the game is great, or you take another box off the shelf...

More than 600 new games are released in Essen each year. Of these, 20 of them end up on your shelf. *Escape, Terra Mystica, Tzolk'in, Robinson Crusoe, Suburbia, Love Letter, Space Cadets - to mention but a few. And what about Mage Wars? Legendary? Descent 2.0? Netrunner? Star Wars: X-Wing Miniatures Game? CO_2? Lords of Waterdeep?*

This is crazy.

There is no room for second chances. Games that were 'meh' the first time around just don't stand a chance. The queue of great games is just too long...

***

I am happy I gave *Netrunner* a second, third and fourth chance. I am happy that I was stubborn and tried again and again. I am happy that after improving my game play and carefully reading all the rules, I finally find this game fun.

What can I say. Withstand the pressure of those new titles. Be stubborn. Play a game a few times before you finally decide it sucks and grab a new one off the shelf...

ONE RULE TO RULE THEM ALL

I have this rule, '*Never acquire a new game if the one you bought previously is still unplayed*'.

It helps me keep my expenditure under control. It helps me maintain a reasonable number of games in my collection. It is important to follow the rules in life.

So - *never purchase a new game if the one you bought previously is still unplayed.* It's clear. Of course, I had to make a small exception when Christmas was approaching, but well, what could I do?! Should I not buy games for my family because I was lame and hadn't managed to play a game I had just bought back in November? Should I hurt them? Obviously the answer here is 'No'.

Basically, the rule is: '*Never acquire a new game for myself if the one I bought previously is still unplayed.*

Now it's fair. It is important to follow the rules.

***

For a moment I wondered if purchasing six games for Christmas wouldn't be a violation of my rule, but technically it wasn't. I was buying them as a single buy, and I was not buying them for myself but for my family. I didn't think it was me exploiting the rules. I hope you agree.

**

There was a tough moment at the beginning of January when there was a great offer for *Smash Up* in one of the Polish game stores. But I needed to look at the situation from a broader perspective – there was still *Space Cadets,* which I had bought for Christmas and hadn't played yet. This is a game for 3-5 players. Merry and I make 2 players.

Honestly, this was the reason I hadn't played Space Cadets yet. I simply couldn't. I really wanted to, but I couldn't.

In this situation everything is clear - *Never purchase a new game for myself if there is a game I have purchased previously that is still unplayed, but only if I could have actually played it.*

Sorry *Space Cadets,* but I was totally allowed to buy *Smash Up.*

**

Mid-January reveals me as a loyal customer and a man of honor. I was contacted by my favorite game store in Poland. They informed me that they had just managed to import the game *Coup,* which I had been asking about a few months earlier. It was difficult to find, but they had managed!

You cannot expect me to be rude and cancel my order, right?

This is a matter of rules. This is a matter of being an honest and responsible man. You have to have rules in life, right?

I bought *Coup,* but I didn't feel I had broken any rules. Anyway, read them carefully. Everything is according to the rules.

Never acquire a new game for myself if the one I bought previously is still unplayed, but only if I could have actually played it, or the pre-order was made earlier and was legit at that moment in time.

***

A few days ago I discovered a problem with the wording of the rule, and as we all know, wording in rules is extremely important. Carelessly I had used the word 'acquire' when I was writing the rule. It obviously should have been 'buy'.

This is important, because the fact that I am just about to receive four new games from the math trade for Polish board games is totally unconnected. Technically, it is not buying. I need you to understand what I'm saying. This is not against the rules. These four new boxes are totally legit.

Never buy a new game for myself if the one I bought previously is still unplayed, but only if I could actually have played it, or the pre-order was made earlier and was legit at that moment of time.

The math trade is legal. I can exchange as many games as I want!

***

This week I bought *Mage Wars.*

If you look at the discount I was offered and if you consider that I am a father of a big family and I am on a really tight budget so I can buy warm clothes for my little kids and...

Okay, you know what? Give me a break! I am a game designer, not a rules lawyer. Are we clear?

Stronghold - prototype stage.

WITH ME YOU ONLY NEED TWO MINUTES BECAUSE I'M SO INTENSE

In 'my version' of *Robinson Crusoe* setup for 4 players was: *Take 2 <u>Starting item</u> cards and 2 <u>No starting item</u> cards. Shuffle them. Deal 1 card to each player.*

This is how players have had fun since the very beginning of the game - it was just like in those novels - they are on the beach and they are checking their pockets looking for something of use. Some of them have something, some of them don't.

It didn't make it into the final rules set.

Why not?

Because it makes set up longer. Because my job is to find all those small moments that make the game longer and nuke them.

Make it fast. As fast as you can.

***

Have you watched The Dice Tower best co-ops? Do you watch or read stuff from other reviewers? Every reviewer presents the shorter length of a game as an advantage. It plays quickly. It is plays smoothly. It plays under an hour. You can play two games in a row.

These are all advantages. No doubt about it, right?

***

I talk a lot with my friends from Rebel Games, the biggest games store in Poland. I talk with them to find out what is trendy, what sells well, what customers say about games. I want to be up to date.

Customers always choose a quicker game.

A customer asks for an economic game.

He is recommended two games.

One plays in 2 hours.

The other in 90 minutes.

Guess which one he will buy?

7 Wonders? A civ game that plays in 40 minutes.

1812: The Invasion of Canada? A war game that plays in 90 minutes.

Egizia? A euro you can play in 45 minutes.

Race for the Galaxy? Man, you can play 3 games in a row in 90 minutes...

Yeah, players like games that play fast, right?

***

Whenever I hear about this, though, one question comes to mind. If we are games fans, and if we love playing games, why do we actually want games to play quickly? Shouldn't we be damn happy playing them as long as possible?

Why do we want our fun to be short? ;)

THERE ARE GAMERS WHO DON'T FALL IN LOVE WITH MY GAMES. CAN YOU BELIEVE IT!?

Last weekend I spent in Bremen, demoing my games during the Bremer Spiele Tage. I think this is a good moment to talk about people playing my games at cons...

Category I

He comes to my stand. I explain the rules. He plays. After the game is finished he gets up from the table, says, 'Thank you' and walks away.

I can't believe this really happened. I want to scream!

Hey! You've just played my game! My great game! How is it possible you didn't fall in love with it? Why didn't you buy a copy? Don't you want to have it in your game collection? Are you kidding me? 'Thank you'? That's it? You just walk away?! C'mon, man!

Category II

He comes to my stand. I explain the rules. He plays. He likes it. He asks, 'Are you the author?' I say, 'Yes, I am.' He says, 'It is a very good game, congratulations.'

I say, 'Thank you!' and I am in heaven.

He says, 'I think I will take one.'

Heaven it is.

Category III

He comes to my stand. I explain the rules. He plays. He loves it. He buys the game. Sometimes he asks for a signed copy. He congratulates me. He walks away.

The next day of the convention I see him coming back. He has brought some friends. He explains the game to them. He recommends it. They buy the game. I say, 'Thank you.'

Heaven? Not heaven. It is paradise...

Bremer Spiele Tage

So I was in Bremen this weekend. There were players who didn't fall in love with my games (can you believe it?!). There were players who played my games, liked them and bought them. There were 'Category III' players too. They played *Robinson* and returned the next day with friends and talked to each other - in German! - about the game. I don't speak German, but I believe they didn't bring their friends just to show them *Robinson* and tell them it sucks, right?

There were even guys who tried to bribe me and buy my last demo copy of the game - my last and incomplete English copy of *Robinson* (greetings to Engoduun and the guys from 'You suck!').

Thank you! It was great to meet all of you. Each con is a great compilation of mini events and meetings that on the one hand boost my ego and keep me in heaven, and on the other hand let me maintain a little bit of humility...

But seriously... How is it possible you didn't fall in love with my...

THIS IS THE STORY!

Last Friday I sent the 8th scenario for *Robinson Crusoe* to my play-testers. As you who played this board game know, *Robinson Crusoe* is in a way a kind of portal to different adventures – each of them deeply inspired by classic adventure stories created by **Jules Verne** or his followers. From the *Castaways* scenario to *Robinson Family,* each scenario was inspired by one of the books or movies in this great genre.

The 8th scenario goes further. It tells an amazing and, more importantly, true story of doctor Livingstone. And I would die, if I couldn't tell you this story...

✳✳✳

David Livingstone (born 19 March 1813) was a Scottish medical missionary and an explorer in Africa. He ran a couple of successful expeditions with a true passion for what he was doing. You can learn more about him and his expeditions by reading history books, but for now just take it for granted – he was The Explorer.

And as you can guess, one day he got into trouble. Big trouble.

He got lost.

Livingstone completely lost contact with the outside world for six years. Only one of his 44 letters dispatched made it to Zanzibar. This one surviving letter to Horace Waller reads: 'I am terribly knocked up but this is for your own eye only, ... Doubtful if I live to see you again ...'

This one letter made it back to the civilized world. It was frightening, and frightening stuff always makes for a good story. That's where the **New York Herald** and the young journalist **Henry Morton Stanley** come in...

***

When Livingstone's letter was publicly presented, the **New York Herald** announced that they were sending an expedition to find and rescue doctor Livingstone. And it was going to go live...

Today we have all types of reality shows, from Big Brother, Real Housewives of Miami to MTV's True Life. In 1871 they had their very own reality show. It was called **Tracking doctor Livingstone.** Every single week the New York Herald published a report written by Henry Morton Stanley sent right from Africa with a description of his adventures and the progress of his rescue expedition. They were looking for Livingstone. They had the story!

A few months ago, when I was reading the biography of Jules Verne, I came upon something I found profoundly interesting. The story of tracking doctor Livingstone was so popular at that time and the New York Herald got so much attention and increased their sales by so much, that the editor of the magazine actually ordered Stanley not to find Livingstone too soon! Stanley visited many different parts of the region, writing dreadful stories of his journey, and kept the story alive for many months.

An awesome tale, don't you think?

Finally, he found doctor Livingstone...

***

So you can imagine. You are in the heart of Africa. You have found a village. There is a white man there. The only white man in this region, and when I call it a region, I mean thousands of thousands of square miles. It is the town of Ujiji on the shores of Lake Tanganyika, 10 November 1871. Clearly this is the end of the expedition. Clearly you have just found Livingstone. What does Stanley do in this situation? He approaches Livingstone and says the words that will become one of the most famous quotes in American journalism: 'Dr. Livingstone, I presume?'

It is always good to remember about etiquette, right?

***

The 8th scenario for *Robinson* tells this story. You are part of a rescue expedition. You need to find doctor Livingstone.

Keep this story in mind when you play it. Let us honor these two great explorers of the nineteenth century!.

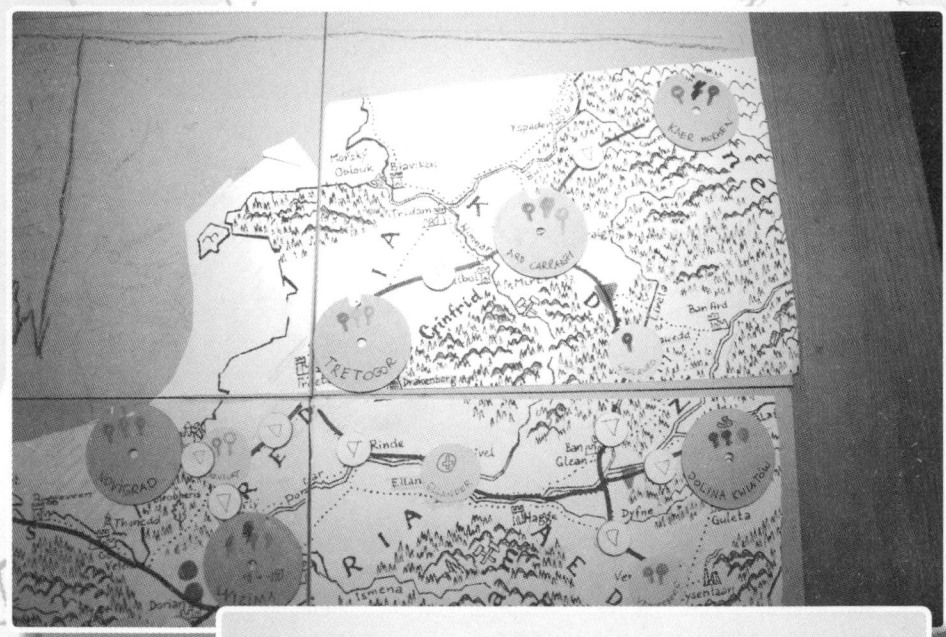

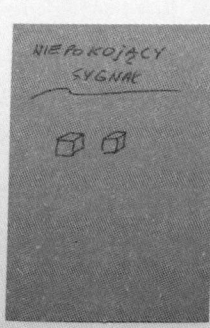
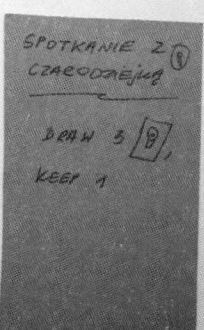

The Witcher prototype.

THERE IS NO LIMIT FOR ME...

We are visiting friends. The kids are bored. We've just finished playing Hands Up. The kids kind of liked it, but don't want to play it again. Olek and Nina go to the other room. Our youngest kid, Lena, stays and wants to play again.

Our friends have no games for kids. But please, worry not! This is not a problem. I am a game designer. I look around in search for some components I can use. I find a d6. Fair enough.

'Highest wins!' I say to Lena. I take the die, I roll 2. Lousy me. Lena takes the die and throws it up very high, almost destroying our friends' chandelier. The die lands a few meters away, next to the sofa, and rolls under it. 'I won!' shouts Lena and runs to find the die under the sofa. She is so damn happy.

Yeah, highest wins...

Merry is shaking with laughter. Lena wants to play again. The chandelier sways dangerously. I think I'd better come up with a different game...

***

Every time I think I can't suck more in terms of presenting rules and writing rulebooks, I prove I actually can. Yes, I can suck more.

There is no limit for me.

ITALIANS, EMOTIONS AND TRZEWICZEK, WHO BELIEVES HE CAN FLY...

Before I became a blogger and before I became a board game designer, it isn't a boast to say that I was quite a famous Role Playing Games writer and Game Master in Poland.

The short story I will present to you today takes place around 2004 in Gliwice. It is a few months after publishing *Neuroshima RPG*, and we are testing our new game called *Monastery RPG*. In short, this is a dark fantasy game, a kind of crossover between Alexander Dumas' novels and the H.P. Lovecraft legacy. The world of the game looks more or less like France in the 1660s, with a huge amount of dark magic, occult etc.

The players play the roles of noble heroes.

So we play. The players play nobles, they role play all the etiquette forms, and use all the good manners in dialogue and honorifics...

I add more and more tension to the game, revealing the first plot elements, and introducing the first problems. Tension slowly builds. I add new elements to the picture, fleshing out the problem that the players will have to face during the game. They talk. 'My dearest sister, I am so glad that we finally meet here in our ancestors' palace', 'My beloved brother, your invitation was so beautifully written – I read and reread the letter for weeks.'

Crap. Boring. Etiquette and honorifics. Meh.

So I add new details to the story. I introduce new elements. The tension rises.

'Dear sister, I am afraid to have to tell you that we need to bla bla bla...'

'My beloved brother, you know you can ask me for any favor. I'd be happy to help you, bla bla bla...'

Yeah, role playing nobles is quite boring. So again I spice things up by leaking the upcoming events to the player who is the 'brother'.

He finally gets what's going to happen soon. He sees where we are headed. He says:

'My dearest sister, I will have to ask you to do me a favor. It will be very difficult for you and you will not like it.'

'My beloved brother, you know you can ask me for anything,' she says.

Uhm, yeah, just let him finish now, darling, I think, and I wait for the 'brother player' to say what he has to say...

'My dearest sister, I need to ask you to leave military school tomorrow, before you take your final exam.'

'You have got to be f'ing kidding me. No f'ing way!' she replies.

Yeah, she might have forgotten about the role playing etiquette at this point. I think that the tension has finally reached the right height.

The girl who is roleplaying the sister doesn't give a shit about roleplaying her character anymore. She is so pissed off, that she doesn't care about such crap as honorifics. The emotions have taken control of the player.

That was my job as a Game Master when running Role Playing games: adding tension, causing emotions to run high. And I know I was kind of good at this.

***

I mention this little story because providing tension is part of my job these days too and when I was in Modena I had a few amazing moments with players and their emotions.

[And yes, this is true, Italians are some of the most emotional people I have ever seen and this is awesome]

For most of the demos of *Robinson Crusoe* that I did during the convention in Modena players were very kind to me. I assisted them for most of the game and they spoke in English with each other even though at times it was hard for them. They could have spoken Italian among themselves - it would have been much easier for them - but they felt it was perhaps rude and tried to speak in English.

That was very kind, allowing me to listen to their plans and discussions and their doubts about what to do next.

But...

But during every single game of *Robinson*, at some point in the game, the amount of important decisions they had to make, the level of pressure the game had built up, the number of doubts and questions about the future reached a point where they ceased to pay attention to me. They didn't give a shit about me not understanding a single word anymore. They didn't care about being rude or not, or about speaking in front of me in a language I don't understand.

They just tried to survive. They were living the game. They were arguing. They were waving their hands. They were moving action pawns from one space to another, back and forth. And they didn't notice me anymore.

At one point this reached a ridiculous level. They had this adventure card, and suddenly one of the players turns to me and speaks to me in Italian.

'Man, I don't speak Italian,' I say.

'Oh, sorry,' he says and raises his hand in apology, 'I was asking if we really have to discard food.'

'I have no idea what adventure card you have. You read this card in Italian!' I tell him.

'Oh, yeah, sorry.' He passes me the card.

I read it.

'Yes, I'm afraid you have to. I am sorry.'

He shouts something in Italian to the rest of players, then he turns back to me, says something to me - in Italian! - and then again shouts something to the other players. He is there, back again. Back on the Island. Trying to survive. Not realizing I am sitting next to him, not realizing we are in Modena, not realizing we are at a convention. He is there, on the Island.

***

Playing with Italian players was an amazing adventure for me. I was there, sitting with them, not understanding a single word, just watching their pure emotions. Seeing them waving their hands, speaking very quickly, looking to the ceiling with an expression on their faces, shouting: 'God, why?!'

With every turn the tension increased, they were struggling more and more. I didn't understand what they were saying, but I could feel what was going on, though. I could feel this pure adventure experience they were having. I was there, sitting at the table, watching people having a great time with my game. I didn't understand the words, but I saw the emotions.

And I have to say, during all those hours I was sitting there, I was the happiest man on the planet.

BOOMERANG EFFECT

I have never had a boomerang, but I have always believed it to be extremely cool. You throw it and sooner or later it returns to you. Well, at least that's what I saw when I was a kid and watched cartoons. Has anyone here tried it in real life?

This week something 'boomerang style' happened.

In 2012 I published *Robinson*. I spent countless hours designing the game and finally it got released. Released into the world. I received feedback very quickly, the first ratings on BGG, the first reviews, emails from players and meeting them at conventions. That was awesome. Every hour, every night, every weekend spent on *Robinson* did pay off. Every time I receive a geekmail from a player of *Robinson*, every time I meet players at a convention I feel that it has all been worth it.

You know all of that. I write about this on my blog all the time.

This week, however, something extraordinary happened. A new scenario for *Robinson* was published. A scenario designed by the game's fans. This was like a hit, a true boomerang experience. I released the game and now it is returning with new content. Amazing content, to be precise.

I may be one of the best writers among board gamers, but this time it is hard to fully express my feelings about that unique experience. Reading great content created by fans for my game. Priceless, as Mastercard marketeers would say.

This may well be the very first time I will just shut up and, instead of talking, I will do something else. I will act. Here is my idea.

This weekend, May 11, I am going to play *Robinson*. I will play it for the first time in my life just for fun. I will not test any new stuff. I will not balance it. I will not run a demo game. I will play it for pure fun. For the very first time in my life.

Please, join me on this day and play *Robinson*. Take your copy off the shelf and play The Naturalist scenario. Let's play it worldwide, as many of you as possible. I will be on twitter for the whole day (@ trzewik) and I will report how many points I managed to get. Look for the #naturalist hashtag.

Let us all say: 'Good work, thanks!' to the team who developed The Naturalist scenario. This is an amazing gift I was given.

May 11. I will be there, on the Island. Be there with me..

TRAPS HIDDEN IN TRAPS

When I first heard about the fact that *Avalon* is different from *The Resistance* because one card (the Merlin character) has been added, I shrugged and sighed in resignation. 'Merlin, novelty my ass,' I thought. Then came the time to analyze the rules and the first signs of rebellion against the new rule. 'What nonsense!', I complained. 'The good characters are playing the game, analyzing, trying to figure out who is a Mordred servant, and then bam!, the bad guys kill Merlin, the end, the good guys have lost!'

Yeah. I didn't like the rule. Before we move on – a short explanation of the rules.

During a game of *Avalon* players are divided into two teams, Arthur's loyal knights and traitors serving Mordred. The identity of the players is a secret. Each of the players only know their own identity, the rest they have to guess or deduce during the game.

Merlin is a special character. The player who is Merlin knows the identity of the traitors. Right from the beginning he knows exactly who serve Mordred... This is a huge advantage for the good guys, so there is a balancing mechanism - at the end of the game the traitors have the right to attack Merlin. If they guess who among the good guys is Merlin, they kill him. If Merlin dies, evil triumphs...

I didn't like it at all. This was a stupid finale of the game. Even so, I decided to give it a try. Soon after, it turned out that I am a complete idiot.

What do we know at the beginning? We all realize that Merlin should not do anything to reveal himself. If the bad guys figure out his identity, they will kill him at the end of the game and they will win. Merlin should play subtly and not attract attention.

Well, unless he plays 'va banque'. He plays 'sheriff style' and he is hoping that the bad guys will think that no Merlin is stupid enough to play so openly! They will think he is just pretending to be Merlin and that someone else is Merlin.

Well, unless one of the good guys attempts to get the attention of the bad guys and pretends to play carelessly, pretending to unintentionally reveal himself... Yeah, then the bad guys will kill him and that is how Merlin is saved!

Unless, a player who is Merlin will play like a moron to steer away the attention of the bad guys. He will make bad decisions and will judge the wrong players during the game, just to 'accidentally' save the good guys at the key moment of the game?

Or maybe...

It turned out that in practice the Merlin's rule works superbly well and gives you extra room for bluffing, setting traps in traps. It adds tons of tension.

And I... well ... What can I say... I have to apologize to Don Eskridge. I apologize that I lost faith in his talent and that I complained about the game before I even played it.

Mr. Eskridge, I'm a jerk.

REAL GAME!

This Monday I played a game that was stuck on my shelf for about three months. It was patiently waiting while I was working on Portal Games prototypes and had no time to play for fun (how stupid does that sound, right?!). Finally I said: 'I am sick of prototypes. I want to play a real game!'

So I played. It was a very strange experience. In my opinion this game was a box full of mistakes. The guys who designed it broke so many design rules that I basically just couldn't believe it. Really.

#1: Cards

Okay, I know, this might not be a general design rule. This is my personal taste. I believe that cards should be in one's hand or open on the table. That's it. Cards are not pawns. Cards are not counters. Cards are not ideal for moving around on the table, being placed under each other and all that kind of stuff.

That is why I don't play *Summoner Wars* (do I see rocks incoming?), that is why I don't play *Innovation* (more rocks?), that is why I don't play *Glory to Rome* (please, stop it, guys!).

I say - keep your cards in hand or put them on the table and DON'T TOUCH THEM. Keep them that way!

On Monday I had to move my cards, I had to put some cards on my cards, and some cards under my cards, and even some cards next to my cards and then I had to move all of my cards, except this one card that is unmovable...

You have got to be kidding me...

#2: Keywords

You put keywords into games to underline some of the most important rules or traits. They are used mostly in CCG games. You might know *Skirmish* in LotR TCG, *Deadly* in GoT, or *Hero* in Invasion... You know them. Keywords.

If you use two hundred and twenty four keywords in your game, these are no longer keywords. These are painwords.

What was Frozen? Man, I don't know. Can you check Taunted again? And Elusive. And, ah, no, no, Fast I do remember. Fast was +1 movement. But in that case... What the hell is a Charge?!

Each card in this game has a few keywords! And there are four or more pages in the rulebook listing all the keywords in the game. Madness. Have you guys heard about making games player friendly? How can you explain the game to new players? How can you start playing the game without it feeling like torture?

Flying. Natural. Regeneration. Burning...

#3: Downtime

I mean, lots of words have been said about making games fast, efficient, making turns or rounds as quick as possible. Every designer wants his game to work smoothly, to play quickly.

In this game, the player – during his turn – chooses two cards from his whole deck. He literally has 50 or so cards in hand and he chooses two of them.

I could not believe this was real. But it was.

#4: Conclusion

I could probably go on and talk about 9 or 6 tokens, short action and long action problems, a huge, grey board, and small cubes for mana points... There are lots of things here that contradict all modern design rules.

I can be honest about this - if the authors of this game came to me during the prototype stage, I would kick their ass and I would show them the door. There is no way I would publish this game.

The problem is, I would be wrong. Because *Mage Wars* is an amazing game.

I had a great time this Monday. It turned out that I can stand moving cards. It turned out that I can learn all these bloody keywords. It turned out I can even get used to this sad, grey board.

I can do this because despite breaking all those game design rules, despite being extremely player unfriendly, *Mage Wars* at its core is pure fun.

That's exactly what I expect from games. So here is my message to designers: Forget about design rules. Go with pure fun. Just like *Mage Wars* did.

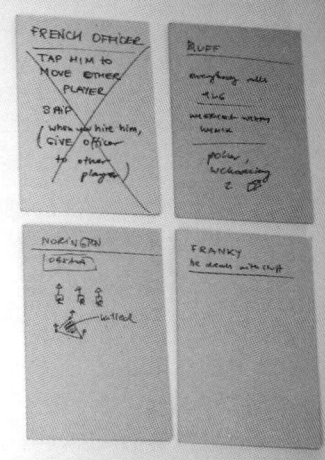

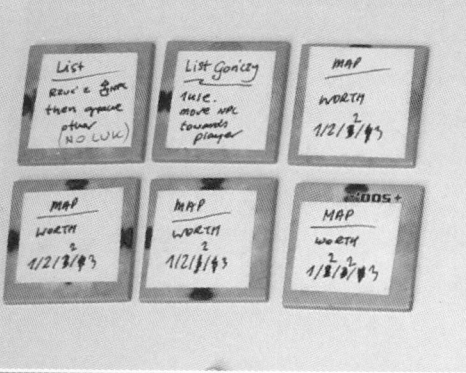

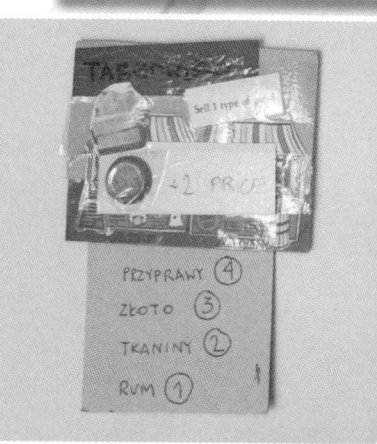

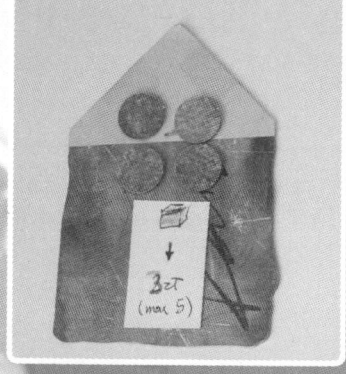

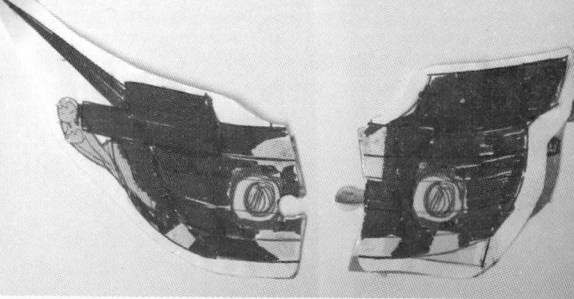

Rattle, Battle, Grab the Loot prototype.

SHE FOLLOWED TOM VASEL'S ADVICE!

The Dice Tower recorded a video called: Top 10 essential games every gamer should have. This is bad. This is so bad. This will kill us. The Dice Tower clearly did not think twice about this. I just want to scream.

Don't you realize what impact this video can have on our lives? Do you think our wives don't watch YouTube?! Are you kidding us?! Wake up!

You don't have to be a prophet to see our wives watching it and then trashing our collection leaving us with only those 10 games!

'This is all you'll need, darling. The guys from The Dice Tower say so.'

I can already see the headlines: 'Her husband had more than 300 board games, but now he has only 10! She followed Tom Vasel's advice.'

***

Guys, you need to record another video. As soon as possible. Here is a script:

Zee: Hi folks. There's been a misunderstanding.

Tom: A huge one!

Sam: We want to apologize to all the wives...

Zee: ...and gamers out there!

Tom: Our latest episode was about the essential 10 games to have in your collection...

Sam: ...meaning 'the best start for your collection'.

Zee: These 10 games are the foundation...

Tom: The foundation, but not the whole building.

Sam: The beginning, not the end...

Zee: You start with them and then you build up your collection.

Tom: It's fine to have more games than 10.

Zee: It's totally fine!

The Dice Tower please act. Clean up the mess you made. Save us before it is too late...

ABOUT MICHIEL, THE GUY WHO HAD A STRONG GUT FEELING…

Last year, when I was writing about Sunday at Essen I told you about my problems with prototypes and that I couldn't play them. Today's post is a follow up to that story.

So as I was saying there was this author who agreed to give me his prototype and…

Okay, just in case you don't remember what I wrote 10 months back, here is a link…

http://boardgamegeek.com/blogpost/14725/essen-behind-scene-part-3-final

***

Long story short – I did set up meetings with young authors, but it turned out that I was very busy and I could not play. I had to apologize and cancel all my playing sessions. I felt like a dick. Guys came to me and I had to tell them, 'Sorry, I cannot play your prototype.' This sucked. I felt terrible. I promised them I would play those prototypes as soon as I reached Poland. I promised it and I really meant it.

So when I got home, I contacted my gaming friends and gave one prototype to each of them. 'Read the rules,' I said. 'Teach me how to play. I need to play it next week. This is an urgent matter.'

I was resting after the fair, but my friends were learning how to play those prototypes. A few days after Essen I was ready and able to play them.

***

It is Wednesday afternoon. My friend Grzesiek comes to my office with one of the prototypes. It is a card game. He sets up the game. He explains the rules. The theme doesn't sound interesting to me, but well...We play. After a few rounds it turns out that the theme makes sense. And the game? I really like it.

Finally we finish. We played the 3 player variant. 'What do you think?' I ask.

'I like it.' says Grzesiek.

'I like it too,' says Piechu.

'It may be a great game when polished,' I say.

I am excited. I really had a good time playing it. Grzesiek is cleaning off the table, but I stop him. 'I'll take it,' I say and I take the prototype home. I want to show it to my Merry.

***

Here is the thing – Merry hates prototypes. She is sick of them. She has had enough of playing my prototypes. When she sees an unpublished game, she runs away.

But that afternoon I don't care. I am so damn excited. I want to show her this card game immediately. I take the prototype home, knowing that Merry will resist, but I want to play it again and I want to play it with her.

So I make Merry play it.

And yes, she loves it too. We play twice that evening. 'Will you publish it?' she asks. 'I will,' I say and I turn on my laptop to contact the author of the prototype.

***

I log in to BGG. I find the page dedicated to this prototype.

Awarded with Ducosim Boardgame Design Prize Contest 2009. Well, I am not surprised.

High ratings. Well, I am not surprised.

The author just found a publisher. Well, I am... what?! WHAT?! WHAT?!

'There is good hope there will be positive news with regard to publication in the nearby future,' says the author in the forum section. I look at the date of the post. Oct 30 2012. That means it was posted the day before. After Essen. Shit.

I am devastated.

I stare at the screen of my laptop and I cannot believe it. The great evening with this amazing card game has turned into the worst evening ever. Merry sees something is wrong. I am pale as a ghost. 'What's wrong?' she asks. 'He has found a publisher,' I say. Silence in our living room.

I mean, I was so close. I had the author at my booth. I had a meeting set up. If only I could have played it that Sunday I would have had this game. I had it in my hands and I let it go. I will regret it for years.

Anyway, I write a geekmail to the author. I congratulate him on the great game. I congratulate him on finding a publisher. I wish him success with his great card game.

I go to bed. That evening sucked.

***

The next morning I receive a geekmail from the author. He writes (and I quote): *'Thank you very much Ignacy! When I was writing about the positive news in regard to the publication, I was writing about you and your Portal Games. I had this strong feeling that you would like the game...'*

If – at this very moment – this guy had been standing next to me, I would have killed him. I am serious. His dead body would be lying next to my desk.

Luckily, he was not there, so I did not kill him. And today I can start this series of articles about *Legacy*, an amazing card game that **Portal Games** has the honor to publish this year. But before we go into details about *Legacy* and the stories about developing this game, I would like to ask you guys for a favor.

Please. Don't ever do this again. No gut feelings anymore, okay? A few more young authors with a strong gut feeling and your beloved publisher will kick the bucket.

IT'S ALL ABOUT TRUST

So here is the situation – I liked the game and I wanted to publish it. Michiel liked Portal Games and he wanted to get his game published.

Could we then sign a contract and move on to publishing stuff, order artwork and start talking with the manufacturer about production?

No, we couldn't.

Before we signed a contract, I had to ask Michiel a very import_ant question. I sent him an email. It went more or less like this...

***

I want you to know, that once the contract is signed, I own your game. I will change it and I will not negotiate with you about changes. I will inform you about them, I will inform you about the reasons I made these changes, but I will not discuss them.

I will not ask you for permission. I am the publisher, not a negotiator.

I don't care if you liked the event deck. If it sucks, I will remove it and I will resist your complaints. I don't care if you like the look of the player board in your prototype. If it doesn't work, I will remove it and I will resist your complaints.

I will take your game and I will change it. Are you prepared for that?

Play Portal Games titles. Play Neuroshima Hex, play Stronghold, play Robinson. And then ask yourself a question – Do these guys know their job? Can I trust them? Can I give them my beloved gem and see them redesigning it?

Michiel, please look at my games. This is my curriculum vitae. If you want me to work on your game, if you want me for this job, sign a contract. Sign a contract and start to cry because I will take your game and I will destroy it.

***

This is how it works guys. Publishers know their market. Publishers know what sells best. Publishers know what players demand. And what is most import_ant... The publisher puts his money on the table. He prints the game. It costs a lot. The publisher has to have the full right to decide on the final product.

So here is the question. Yes, question for all of you who submit your games to publishers! Are you ready for that? Can you give me your game and leave it behind? It is a tough decision...

***

Michiel signed the contract. So I took his game and I tore it to pieces...

TRASH IT

Trash story #1: Dowry

Every Friend card in *Legacy* has its cost. It represents the cost of marriage. In terms of rules it tells you how much you have to pay for putting this card into play. For some marriages you pay more, for some you pay less. A simple mechanism. It worked well.

But... One day I asked a question...

'In the old days the father of a daughter had to bring a dowry to a marriage. We don't have that here, do we?'

'No, we don't,' said Walec.

He didn't know what was coming...

'I think it would be really cool if we did have that. If the player has a daughter, he wants to give her a husband - he will pay a dowry. If the player has a son, he wants to find him a good wife - he will expect to receive a dowry...'

Walec looked at me with fear in his eyes. At this point he probably realized what was coming. Quickly I confirmed his fears...

'I want all female Friend cards in the game to have no cost value. Instead, I want them to have an income value that will represent the dowry your family received. When you marry your son, you will receive money.'

Walec knew that to protest would be useless, but he had to give it a shot.

'Ignacy, the entire economy of the game will be ruined then. We will have to recalculate every damn friend card, every single action in the game, every single mission, patron, everything... We will need to correct it all from scratch. And it is not only the prices which will change, the entire economy of the game will change if players can earn money with the marriage action - this will become a completely new strategy...'

I knew all of that.

'Can you recalculate all of that?' I asked without a blink.

'Michiel had 3 years to calculate the costs and the worth of the cards and the actions and balance it all...'

'So we will work faster. We have 6 months...'

That day we took the entire economy of the game and simply trashed it.

Trash story #2: Crystal ball

In the prototype stage there was an action called *Crystal ball*. It let you draw *2 child cards* and choose one of them. Thematically it represented the head of the family visiting the fortune teller and asking about the gender of a child about to be born.

But there was a serious problem with this action - it was not worth an Action pawn. At some point we even made it free, no money to pay, all you had to do was spend an action - but still, too expensive. An action pawn is damn valuable in *Legacy*.

So I removed this action from the game. It was less popular than the other actions, so I decided to trash it.

As you can imagine, soon after that players started to complain. 'I have 4 daughters! I need a son! I need help! Bring back the crystal ball!'

'Oh, come on!' I resisted 'Deal with it! I will not bring it back!'

Unfortunately, Michiel was missing this action too. 'Players need to have the chance to choose the gender of a child. It is important to be able to create the right genealogical tree. It is important for strategy.'

'I know,' I replied to his emails.

'Will you bring back the crystal ball?'

'No.'

'What will you do then?'

'I don't know.'

Months passed. No Crystal ball. No alternative either. The well of ideas on how to solve this problem had gone dry.

But Michiel didn't give up. He sent another email, this time to Walec: 'At that time doctors said that if you cut off one testicle...'

Walec received this email and he started to laugh. He read it out loud.

Quote:

An 18th-century French book called The art of boys suggested an extreme method of ensuring children of one sex. The author suggests that one testicle and one ovary are intended for each sex. By removing a testicle or ovary, children of the other sex can be guaranteed.

'This is good,' I said.

Walec stopped laughing. Looked at me. 'What? What is good?'

'This is good,' I said again. 'The player can draw from the child deck as long as it takes for him to draw a daughter, but since the father lost a testicle, he loses an Honor. This is brilliant.'

'You have got to be kidding.'

'Why?'

'You actually want to introduce a rule that lets you cut off a testicle?!'

'Blend rules with theme. That is what we do here. I tell you, Michiel will love it! Add the removal of a testicle into the rules and start testing!'

Is there any other game here on BGG that lets you do this?

Trash story #3: Full bin

For the past few months we have changed the game a lot. We trashed the event deck, we designed and then trashed special skills for Mansions (they will be back as goodies for pre-orders!), we designed a new action (Lands) and we trashed it after a few weeks, we designed the War action and...

Ah, the War action!

Yesterday, when I started to write this article, Merry said: 'You have to write about the War cards. It was the dumbest set of rules you have designed for years!'

Yeah, she supports me 24/7.

Anyway, War cards - in the game there were scientists (connected with the Fertility Doctor action), aristocrats (connected with the Acquire a Title action), craftsmen (connected with the Venture action), artists (connected with the Mansion action), diplomats (connected with the Mission action)... and there were officers - connected with no action.

Eurogamers don't like it that way, do they?

So together with Multidej I decided to design the War action. You could send your son to war. I designed a deck of about 40 cards and believe me, they were awesome.

Your son could become hero and gain Prestige.

Your son could become a captive and you would need to pay money to rescue him.

Your son could get wounded and could not have children anymore.

Your son could find a beautiful foreign girl and you would receive 1 of 10 friend cards...

Your son could...

It was an adventure deck. I love adventures. I was designing and designing new war cards and I had so much fun.

And then we played it.

One player's son received royal honor after an epic battle. The player got 3 Honor points.

Another player's son got killed. The player discarded his card.

'Are you f... kidding me?' the player asked.

'You know, you sent him to war. What were you expecting?' I was trying to defend the action, but it was useless. The randomness in this deck was crazy.

I changed this deck around, adapting the cards, for a couple of weeks, trying to make it less random, but in the end it was always clear – the War deck is an adventure deck. *Legacy* is not an adventure game.

So I took all those amazing cards and threw them into the bin...

Trash story: conclusion

I was writing about it last year when I was posting about Vlaada Chvatil destroying *Robinson* - designing games is basically trashing stuff. You trash stuff all the time. No mercy for your beloved ideas. Every single day you are looking for a better solution and that is all that counts.

By introducing the dowry rules and changing the entire economy of the game we took upon ourselves a crazy amount of work. It was a damn hard decision. But we did it because we believed it would make Legacy a better game, with more strategies and better theme.

A few weeks ago I was in Hungary. I was running a demo game of *Legacy*. When Simon (if I remember correctly) drew a third daughter card in a row he literally began to cry. Having three daughters is like announcing bankruptcy.

'Man, you need to start a venture,' we said.

He burst into tears.

This one moment of pure fun and joy, with the theme so nicely incorporated, and us poking fun at that one player who had 3 daughters which would cost him so much money... It was worth spending all those days and nights recalculating every single card....

ZOMBI

Zombiak. Na początku
twojej tury przesuń Zombiaka
o 1 pole do przodu.

TAK SOBIE NA TRZY PLUS

• MISS EXPO •

Zombiak, Na początku
twojej tury przesuń Zombiaka
o 1 pole do przodu.

TAK SOBIE NA TRZY PLUS

ZOMBI

ZOMBIAK. Na początku twojej tury
przesuń Zombiaka o 1 pole do przodu.

OBIE, NA TRZY PLUS

ZOMBI

ZOMBIAK. Na początku twojej
tury przesuń Zombiaka
o 1 pole do przodu.

TAK SOBIE NA TRZY PLUS

ZOMBI

ZOMBIAK. Na początku twojej
przesuń Zombiaka o 1 pole do przodu.

TAK SOBIE NA TRZY PLUS

ZOMBI

ZOMBIAK. Na początku twojej tury
przesuń Zombiaka o 1 pole do przodu.

TAK SOBIE NA TRZY PLUS

ZOMBI

ZOMBIAK. Na początku twojej tury
przesuń Zombiaka o 1 pole do przodu.

TAK SOBIE NA TRZY PLUS

ZOMBI

ZOMBIAK. Na początku twojej tury
przesuń Zombiaka o 1 pole do przod

TAK SOBIE NA TRZY PLUS

Zombiaki anniversary edition - prototype cards.

YOU HAVE 8 WEEKS

I never really did pay too much attention to solo variants for board games. I saw board gaming as a social experience and I rarely thought of it as a way to play alone. None of my previous games had a solo variant (except *51st State* for which I was repeatedly asked by fans to create one, finally designing one).

Then *Robinson* came. Solo play was so deeply ingrained in the theme that I had to design a solo variant. It was not hard. It just worked right from the beginning.

I would have forgotten about it right after releasing the game if not for players who... really played this variant! It turns out everybody recommends it, and people really like it... I started to search the board gaming forums and I learned something – gamers like solo variants. They like it when a game has a good solo variant. This is one of the traits my games should have. A good solo variant.

That was exactly what I told Michiel when we met in Bremen in February 2013. We needed a solo variant.

Michiel said he had no solo variant yet, but he could design one quite easily. *Legacy* has no direct interaction (Okay, it has some, but not too much) and we will only need to simulate the fact that players block each other on the main board. We will have a solo variant, he said.

And that would be true if not for me asking a strange question again...

***

We were in the office. Walec was working on the Friend cards with his desk looking like one big family tree. He was grumbling to himself, changing cards in the tree, taking notes...

'You know what would be cool?' I ask.

That is the phrase that freezes the blood in the veins of my employees. They hate it when I have these 'cool idea' moments.

Walec stops grumbling.

'What?' he asks.

'It would be cool if we could turn it upside down. In the solo variant you could start in the present and then try to discover the truth about your ancestors. You would start with some initial information about your family and you could try to discover the rest and fill in the blank spaces.'

'Yes, that would be cool,' he says with the tone of his voice saying: 'That is a beautiful dream, boss, but don't you even dare think that we could do this!'

I am not good with this whole tone thing.

'I love it already,' I say. 'I can imagine myself sitting at the desk with all these cards and some clues about my family. I can imagine looking for answers and digging in the past. With hot tea, good music, late in the night. That will be the best solo variant ever.'

Walec is in consternation.

'You have 8 weeks,' I say. 'Try to design it that way. If it is impossible, we will pass on it and we will stick with a classic solo variant. But I believe it is worth a shot.'

***

The 8 weeks have passed like a day. We are back in the office. Walec is doing the setup for the solo variant. He is a little bit nervous. He has worked on this variant like crazy and today I will decide if we keep working on it or we cancel it and go back to the basic variant.

'You start here. Here are your parents. You draw these two cards now. These are your first clues. They represent some old documents about your family you found in the attic. Old letters or something like that. Later on you will draw more of these cards, older and older up to the manuscript from the 18th century. Look, this one says your mother had two sisters, and the other one says your grandpa was a famous scientist...'

He explains everything to me and shows me all the available actions, and all these cards he designed, and he talks and talks, with all this information about balance and ideas behind the rules and I can't stop him because he is talkin' damn fast. It turns out that when he is nervous he talks a lot. He speaks so fast, without giving himself time to take a breath, that I am unable to interrupt him.

At some point I know literally everything about this variant. And since the very first sentence I knew it was brilliant - we have a mystery here, some old letters and documents, old family, digging in the past...

I want to tell him that I love this variant and he has the green light to finish and balance it, but I can't say anything because he is still talking like a mad man! This is getting ridiculous.

[You know that feeling, right? You can't stop talking because you are afraid of what you will hear when you are done. So you keep talkin' and talkin'...]

Finally he is done.

'What do you think?' he asks and shuts up.

'I love it,' I say.

***

I want to give credit to Walec. Michiel is the author of the game and he will be on the cover. I am the front-man of Portal Games and I will always be in the spotlight. Walec? He will be mentioned on the last page of the rulebook. Small font. Additional material section. No one will ever know that he did the impossible.

He took the components of *Legacy* and he designed a small mini game for one player. I owe him this post.

HOW I SUMMONED MICHAL ORACZ

I think it was August 2012. I was extremely tired from testing *Robin-son*, playing four or five test games every single day, playing all those six scenarios, all those different cards and player variants. I was low with fuel, exhausted. I honestly dreamed about not playing a proto-type for a year.

One day, in a moment of despair, I called Michal Oracz. The guy who designed *Neuroshima Hex*, then *Witchcraft* and then abandoned game design and turned to his other passions...

So when I understood that I would have no strength to start working on a new prototype for 2013, I decided to make a call and summon him.

***

'Michal, I need help. I did 6 games in the past 4 years, and now I am finishing with *Robinson* and I am sick of playing my prototypes. I need a break. I need an extended vacation. I need you to give me a game.'

'Okay,' said Michal.

He then opened his drawer and visited my office the next day.

'Here is a list of some of the ideas I have,' he said, and passed me two sheets of paper. There were about 40 games listed. Wow. It took me a while to read it.

There were a number of interesting ideas. I asked about the one called Alien. I like Alien. To be honest, who doesn't, right?

Michal grabbed a piece of paper and began to draw...

***

'In all these sf games like *Doom* or *Gears of War*, players are moving miniatures - one moves 3 spaces, then the other guy moves 2 spaces and aims, and then the next guy moves 3 spaces and then the first guy moves again, and they are moving and moving...'

'...what's your point?' I asked.

'I want my Alien to be like *Mall of Horror*,' he said. Michal knows me. He knows that Mall of Horror is in my Top 10 games ever, on the first spot. The best game on the planet.

Yes, he had my attention.

'*Mall of Horror?*'

'Yes, you know, the locations in *Mall of Horror* have rules, you move to Security HQ, and you see where zombies go, you move to Parking and you draw items... There is no *I move three spaces. There is I run to Parking to grab some weapons!*

I want a few locations on this space station and you move between these locations, but there are no small steps. You move from Corridors to Armory, you move from Dock to Bridge, you move from Bridge to Med Lab. Each time you move, it matters.'

I already liked it, but he kept talking:

'You move to the Med Lab sector and you heal all your guys. You move to the Armory and you get a super weapon. You move to the Corridors and you kill an enemy. Huge actions. Every move matters. No: *I move 3 spaces*. I want: *I move to the Armory*. A player's pawns will not represent one soldier, but rather a group. If you move to the

Corridors it means your faction has taken control of the Corridors and you can shoot an enemy. You move to the Med Lab means your soldiers took control of the Med Lab and you can heal now...'

He talked on and on, but there is no need to report all of this. You get the point, right? This movement would be rather abstract, but on the other hand so incredibly thematic. Just like *Neuroshima Hex*, the war game that we all love and play a lot - there are units, battles, HQ and such stuff, but at its core it is a great abstract game.

Michal had this new idea - one space station. A few rooms with powerful abilities. And your faction trapped there with an enemy. Every time you move, you move to a new room and you activate its ability.

'I want this for Essen 2013,' I said.

***

More than a year later I can say: I have it for Essen 2013. It's called Theseus. Michal Oracz is back. I summoned him and we have a great tactical sf game.

And what about me, you might ask? Well, I never did have time for a vacation. Perhaps next year...

.

JUGGERNAUT

Wygrana Molocha: odrzuć wierzchnią kartę z tali Posterunku na stos kart odrzuconych (jest ona widoczna dla obu graczy).

SIŁA **2**

TYP

AKTYWACJA

TYP AKTYWACJA SIŁA

HYBRYDA

2

Wygrana Molocha: odrzuć wierzchnią kartę z tali Posterunku na stos kart odrzuconych (jest ona widoczna dla obu graczy).

HYBRYDA

2

Wygrana Molocha: odrzuć wierzchnią kartę z tali Posterunku na stos kart odrzuconych (jest ona widoczna dla obu graczy).

SOLDIER

LOREM IPSUM DOLOR SIT AMET, CONSECTETUR ADIPISCING ELIT, SED DO EIUSMOD TEMPOR INCIDIDUNT UT LABORE ET DOLORE MAGNA ALIQUA. UT ENIM AD MINIM VENIAM, QUIS NOSTRUD EXERCITATION

TYPE ACTIVATION STRENGHT

★ ▼ 4

SOLDIER

ACTIVATION ▼

STRENGHT 4

LOREM IPSUM DOLOR SIT AMET, CONSECTETUR ADIPISCING ELIT, SED DO EIUSMOD TEMPOR INCIDIDUNT UT LABORE ET DOLORE MAGNA ALIQUA. UT ENIM AD MINIM VENIAM, QUIS NOSTRUD EXERCITATION

JUGGERNAUT

2

Wygrana Molocha: odrzuć wierzchnią kartę z tali Posterunku na stos kart odrzuconych (jest ona widoczna dla obu graczy).

TYPE ACTIVATION STRENGHT

★ ▼ 4

LOREM IPSUM DOLOR SIT AMET, CONSECTETUR ADIPISCING ELIT, SED DO EIUSMOD TEMPOR INCIDIDUNT UT LABORE ET DOLORE MAGNA ALIQUA. UT ENIM AD MINIM VENIAM, 2013 NOSTRUD EXERCITATION

SOLDIER

Neuroshima Convoy second edition prototype c

THESEUS – OR WHY I AM THE WORST TESTER EVER

The first version of *Theseus* was ready very quickly. Michal told me about his idea and he began the design of different locations and cards. He is good at this stuff and he worked quickly and efficiently...

I, on the other hand, had this simple idea with *Mancala* rules. A few days earlier I had played *Trajan* and I really liked the use of the 'mancala wheel' in that game, but in my opinion it lacked something. It lacked interaction. When thinking about the space station for *Theseus* I got this cool idea - we could take the mancala wheel from *Trajan*, but change it a little bit - we would make every pawn matter - no matter whether it was mine or yours - each pawn would change the number of spaces you could move from this location.

I showed it to Michal. It worked perfectly. In a few days *Theseus* was basically ready...

***

For the next few weeks we played Theseus every Wednesday. I was giving Michal my suggestions, asking him to change things, I was looking for the best game play, tweaking the game, and every week he received a long list of changes I wanted him to make to the game.

From my point of view we were doing great.

Unfortunately, it was only my point of view...

***

The thing I did not realized at that time was that Michal is not used to working this way. For me it was an obvious cycle, my daytime practice - change this, change that, move back, don't change this, but change that in a different way, remove the special cards, add different special cards, try to shorten the game, try to make it longer...

This is how I work. I play and I test, I play and I look at what works best. I am not a wise ass. I don't know all the best solutions from the very beginning. I am a testing animal. I play and I play, and I change things as many times as needed until the moment I feel that this is it.

For me, all the changes, moving back and forth, was fun. For Michal it was not fun at all. Every single week he got closer and closer to losing his temper.

So one Wednesday...

***

It was just another testing Wednesday. But Michal that day had a strange look on his face. He was damn serious. He sat down, put his prototype on the table and before he set up the game, he said something like the following:

'I think we are not moving forward. This is pointless. We play and change the game and nothing works. I have made some changes, but if you don't like it today I think I will abandon this project.'

Wow. That was a shock. For the past few weeks I had had a great time exploring the different possible variants of the game and now what?! Abandon the game? Not moving forward? WTF?

'What do you mean?' I asked.

'Let's play. If once again you don't like it, we will talk and we will have to make a decision...'

Okay, that was kind of a shock. I hadn't seen that coming.

So we played. I was quite nervous. It was to be a fun afternoon. But it wasn't! Michal was damn serious. I felt like I was playing with Christopher Walken. This was not cool!

***

I don't know how it is possible. Was it because of the threat that Michal had made at the beginning? Was it because of the fact that he had spent countless hours on this new version? Was it just because everything finally clicked and fell into place...? I don't know. The fact is - that afternoon *Theseus* was working damn well. I really liked it.

I told Michal that. He took the prototype and continued his work.

I am not sure what would have happened if I had suggested another batch of changes. Were his words that Wednesday only a bluff or was he really up against the wall and had he had enough of my contrary suggestions and changes...?

We will never know...

***

We argued a lot over these last 12 months. We had many serious and bloody fights with me accusing Michal that he has no idea about design and with him accusing me that I have no idea about strategy... Fights with me explaining to him that one faction is weaker and with him kicking my ass playing that very faction. Fights with me telling him that the game is too fiddly and with him asking me if I have - by any chance - played *Robinson Crusoe*...

We fought over every single card. We fought over every single rule. It was a one year war.

Both of us loved the game. Both of us wanted to do our best and make this game better. Michal was the author - he had the full authority to make any changes he wanted. I was the publisher and his friend and his loyal tester - I felt I had the full authority to suggest to him any changes I wanted made.

So we both fought for our beliefs.

***

Now, the game is ready. The war is over. I can probably say I was the worst tester ever. I was doing exactly the thing I hate when my testers do it. I was suggesting new rules, I was trying to influence the author, I was pushing my ideas and trying to make *Theseus* my game. I was terrible.

If I had such a tester on my testing team, I would have kicked him off the team after two test games.

Michal was patient. He fought with me for over a year. He kept ignoring most of my ideas and he did his job. He made this game the way he wanted it to be.

Conclusion?

Never ever invite me for testing. And check out *Theseus*. This is an amazing game, even though Michal threw most of my brilliant ideas in the bin....

EXPECT THE UNEXPECTED

In the beginning *Theseus* was called Pandora. We really liked the name, it was easy to remember, it had great connotations with mythology, and it was a widely known word. There was one tiny problem, though - there were already 5 different games with that name in the BGG database.

So we had to find something new. That's how we found *Theseus*.

***

Pandora is an inspiring name. At some point Michal came to the office and told me that he had this idea for a fifth faction. It would be called Pandora.

'It will be a disease,' he said. 'It will grow and affect enemies in nasty ways. This will be a very different, very unique faction.'

Yeah, the idea was cool. But I had to destroy his dream.

'We can't afford a fifth faction in the box. My budget is already very tight. We are aiming for a €36 box. We have unique boards, lots of cards, wooden pawns... There is no way I can add anything else. Keep Pandora for the expansion. We design games for 2-4 players, we will have 4 factions. I cannot add any more cards or boards to the box, sorry.'

Michal said he understood.

We went back to testing the four factions. Weeks passed. Finally we changed the name from Pandora to *Theseus*. I forgot about the fifth faction...

***

One Wednesday Michal came to the office to play-test *Theseus*.

'I have Pandora with me,' he said.

'It's called *Theseus* now. Get used to this name, man!' I said smiling.

'I mean the fifth faction. Pandora. I have it ready,' he said.

'I told you I can't afford it. The production of the game is already very expensive with all of those unique boards.'

'Let me show you,' he said.

He took out a ziplock bag and poured out a few tokens. He looked at me, his eyes shining with pride, and smiled.

'Can your budget handle a few more tokens?' he asked.

'That's it? Just those tokens?' I was truly stunned.

'Yes,' he said.

'And it works?' I couldn't believe he really had created the Pandora faction.

'You will love it,' he said.

***

So here we are. We have a game for 2-4 players with 4 different factions... and we have a fifth faction in the box. It has been added because we have dreams. It has been added because we believe the impossible is possible. It has been added because Michal is a stubborn son of a bitch and wouldn't allow the budget to take control of his game. He spent as much time as needed and used his talent and passion to design a faction that would fit my budget.

We give you more than you expect. We want you to smile when you open the box. We want you think: "These guys at Portal really love their jobs..."

***

Michal and I have a history together - we both have RPG roots. Portal Games was founded in 1999 as an RPG company. Together we wrote a few RPGs, dozens of expansions, and a countless number of articles and adventures for RPGs.

We both love good stories.

However, our approach to board game design is totally different. I design huge, story driven games like *Stronghold* and *Robinson*, which are often too fiddly. He designs quite abstract games like *Neuroshima Hex* and *Witchcraft*, which are very clear.

(What is funny is that we both think that our own games are super thematic.)

At one point, when I was talking with Michal about Theseus I was really surprised with his approach - it seemed like all of the faction cards did not only have rules, but also a story behind them. Michal knew exactly why each card was in the game, not only in terms of rules and balance, but also in terms of story of the particular faction.

He knew exactly what was going on at this space station.

'We should show it to the players,' I said.

'What?' he asked.

'Show them why these factions are on *Theseus* and why they are fighting,' I said.

It took us a few weeks to find a good way to show you this story...

***

Do you know the term 'gamebook'? Have you played or at least heard about *Choose Your Own Adventure or Fighting Fantasy? Played Freeway Warrior* created by Joe Dever?

We have RPG roots. We can tell stories. We can tell you what's going on in Theseus in a really fun way...

***

I must say, it was not easy. I must say, it was much more work than we expected. I must say... I was crazy when I had this idea about writing four short gamebooks, one for each of the four main factions. Four short stories that would reveal the mysteries of *Theseus*. I admit, it was an insane dream. A dream in which I envisioned the back of each faction board hiding a QR code that leads the player to a small PDF file with a gamebook dedicated to that faction...

We didn't have to do it. This is extra effort no one would have expected from any board game publisher. This is something that isn't industry standard, no, we at Portal like to go the extra mile, we want to raise the bar.

We want to add more than you expect. We want to make you smile when you open the box. We want you to think: 'These guys at Portal really love their jobs...'

***

Dear gamers,

Yes, we love our jobs.

I believe that none of you who read this blog doubt that.

Expect the unexpected. And watch us raise the bar.

Ignacy Trzewiczek
Portal Games

ABOUT TESTING GAMES, PART I

Suddenly the door in my office opens and Ryu runs in. 'Did you see?'

'What?' I ask.

'Rosenberg's new game is broken!'

'Bullshit,' I say. Everybody knows Uwe has an army of trusted testers and his games are always perfectly balanced.

'No, really! You check BGG!' he says and goes back to his office.

***

Uwe's game has a small problem, as players have pointed out. Another Essen release, *Cornish Smuggler* has a bigger problem, as players pointed out right after a few plays. In the next few weeks probably more games will have a smaller or bigger problem.

Every year I publish a game, I ask myself the question, 'Did I test this enough? Is there a winning strategy I haven't found? Is there a smart ass somewhere out there who will play my game and find a hole in the rules, exploit it and create a winning combo?'

I fear it every single year...

***

If you listen to interviews with designers who give advice to young authors, most of them, really, say just one thing: Test your games. Test them and test them and then test them again

But not too many designers tell you how exactly you should test your games. Because, you know, testing is not just playing. It is something much more difficult. If you play your prototype and you think you are actually testing it, you are wrong.

In a few short articles I'd like to share my experience regarding this process. I hope you will find it useful.

***

First of all, I have my testers divided into a few very important groups. Depending on the stage of the prototype, I need different feedback. Some testers are better at one type of feedback, while others are better at another.

It took me a while to get to know all those fellow gamers who want to spend time playing my prototypes and help me here. I categorized them, putting them in different baskets and I invite people from a particular basket depending on what I need at that particular moment.

So my first message - don't test with random people. Don't just test with a bunch of gamers. You pick the right people.

Because testing is work.

Because testing is not just playing.

Because you don't need just players.

You need people who will do a job for you.

You need to choose the right people for this job.

***

My Merry is a **silent tester.** I want to say this is the most important type of tester, but let's face it - each type is equally important.

A silent tester just plays. He (or she) is like a living flower, just sitting there, playing, and saying nothing. Just being there.

He doesn't share his brilliant ideas.

He doesn't suggest anything to you

He doesn't comment on the gameplay.

He doesn't ask questions.

And he patiently accepts all changes in the gameplay you introduce in the middle of the game.

You began the game with 1 coin being worth 1 VP, but in the middle you change it to 2 VPs, and later on you decide that coins don't give any VPs at all.

That's fine. No problem for him. A silent tester just plays. He is fine with everything you come up. He sits and plays.

***

You need a silent player in the beginning. The prototype doesn't work, and you know that. Everything is a mess, and you know that. The game doesn't make sense yet, and you know that.

You don't need a tester to tell you all of that. You need a tester to shut his bloody mouth and just play with you.

It is hard to find a silent tester. It is hard to find a flexible player who accepts that the game changes three times within a time span of less than 30 minutes, and yet just shuts up and plays. This is a flexible player who can improvise and follow you like a shadow, with patience. With lots of patience.

Yes, I have such a treasure at home. A lucky bastard I am..?'.

Puma

You find a tiger! You hide. But with no doubt it will run after you... You try to wrong track and you don't go back to camp (execute Weather and Night phase outside camp) or...

SHUFFLE into Event Deck

Puma found you!

Deduct 1 Defence
Deduct 1 Weapon
Strenght 3 (2 Food, 1 Fur)

Draw another card

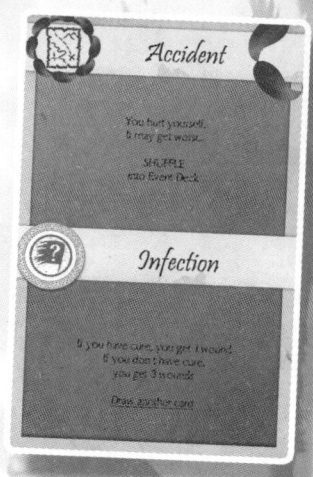

Accident

You hurt yourself.
It may get worst...

SHUFFLE
into Event Deck

Infection

If you have cure, you get 1 wound.
If you don't have cure,
you get 3 wounds

Draw another card

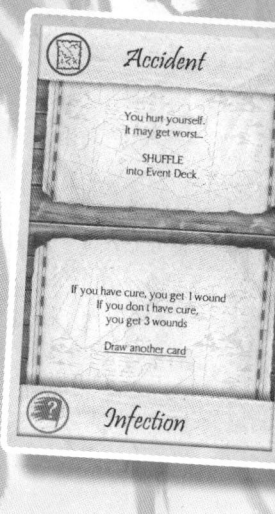

Accident

You hurt yourself.
It may get worst...

SHUFFLE
into Event Deck

If you have cure, you get 1 wound
If you don't have cure,
you get 3 wounds

Draw another card

Infection

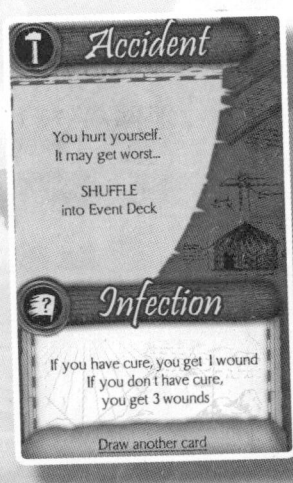

Accident

You hurt yourself.
It may get worst...

SHUFFLE
into Event Deck

Infection

If you have cure, you get 1 wound
If you don't have cure,
you get 3 wounds

Draw another card

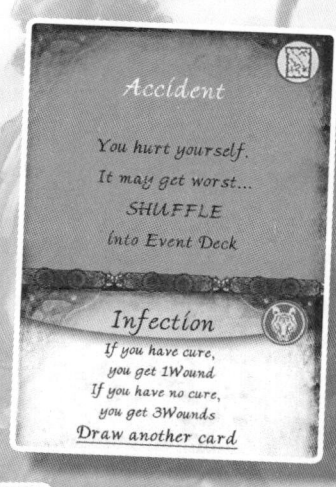

Accident

You hurt yourself.
It may get worst...
SHUFFLE
into Event Deck

Infection

If you have cure,
you get 1Wound
If you have no cure,
you get 3Wounds
Draw another card

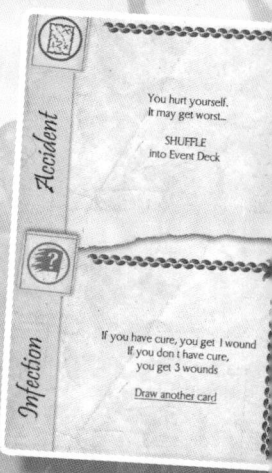

Accident

You hurt yourself.
It may get worst...

SHUFFLE
into Event Deck

Infection

If you have cure, you get 1 wound
If you don't have cure,
you get 3 wounds

Draw another card

Pipe and tobacco

Use twice

Pipe and tobacco

Use twice

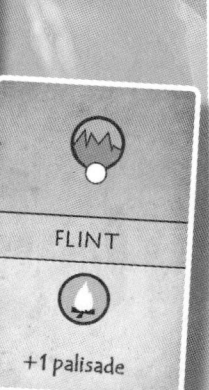

FLINT

+1 palisade

Pipe and tobacco

Use twice

Robinson Crusoe - prototype card

ABOUT TESTING GAMES, PART II

When I am done with **silent tester**, the prototype has its foundations ready. I am more or less satisfied with the prototype. It is time to play with a new breed of testers - the **brilliant idea** testers.

You need guys who have many ideas. They will try to change your prototype into the game they would like. You give them a prototype and you see what they come up with, what they suggest. I prefer to work with silent testers, but yes, there is this moment when you need these guys too. They will overwhelm you with their 'brilliant' ideas.

'It would be cool if in my turn I could do...'

'Hey, what if you added one more...'

'You know, I feel there is this one element missing from your game. Perhaps you could change...'

I hate it. But this is an important part.

They give you ideas, but remember - you have your foundations. You have your armor – an ideas-proof prototype of the game. You know which of the tester's ideas won't work for you. And once in a while an idea will be suggested that really works. You take it. You improve your prototype. You thank the tester.

All the other ideas... discard them without mercy.

Never sit with guys who have their own ideas and who love to share them before you are ready for it, or rather, your game is ready for it. If you don't yet have a foundation, you will be like a flag - you will change your game with every suggestion of the testers. This is bad. You will change, and change and change and not move forward.

Have a base idea.

Then listen to suggestions.

Discard most of them.

Use a few - only those which work with the base.

First the silent tester.

Then the brilliant idea tester.

Then the crazy tester. I will cover the crazy testers next week.

ABOUT TESTING GAMES, PART III

This story takes place in Gliwice, during the winter of 1997. A long time ago. I am at college and of course I am running a games club there. We play RPG and miniatures games every Wednesday and Friday evening. I run a *Warhammer 40K Battle* campaign for more than 10 players, with a huge map of the provinces, with an additional set of rules, with a development system (when you conquer a province you can get magical stuff, gold, soldiers...). We have a great time.

One day the door opens and in the doorway we see a kid. He may be 15 years old. Okay, perhaps 16. A kid. He enters and quietly says something like, 'I heard you can play *Warhammer Battle* here...'

We look at each other and laugh. You know, we were at college and this was a 15 year old kid...

Finally, Tom points his finger at the kid and asks, 'You play? I challenge you! My name is Tom, by the way.'

***

Before we move on, a few words about Tom. I had met him a few years earlier. He was a 'munchkin' style player. He exploited the rules of every single game he played. I met him when I was playing *Doom*

Trooper CCG, then we played *Warhammer Battle,* and after that many other games. He always won. And always broke the system to do that. No remorse. No conscience. No honor.

At the time of the story, Tom was exploiting the rules of my War-hammer campaign. He was playing the Undead army. None of the players in the campaign had magical weaponry yet (because of the development rules they needed to conquer lands with magical weap-ons before they were allowed to use them), so he used the Wraiths regiment in the campaign. Wraiths were immune to non-magical weapons.

Yeah. That kind of player.

That day, when the kid entered our club, Tom had notched up about 10 wins in a row in the campaign and still no f'ing idea about fair play.

So he challenged a kid. He saw it as easy prey.

And you all probably know how the story goes...

***

The following week the kid came to our club with his Wood elves army. He set up his forces and in 20 minutes defeated Tom.

Just like that. Kicked his ass in less than half an hour.

Even today, as I am writing this right now, 17 years later, I am still smiling. That was f'ing amazing.

After 30 minutes it was all over and Tom had been defeated. He couldn't believe what had just happened. The kid was looking at us, not fully understanding why we all had big smiles on our faces. 'Would anyone else like to play with me? It was quite a short match,' he said.

***

How was it possible that he crushed Tom? He had spent some time preparing for the battle and thinking what he could do best. He took on Tom's Wraith regiment with an Elven Wardancers unit, made a special dance and directed all 18 hits at one model - Vampire, the general of the Undead army. Vampire was not a Wraith. Vampire was not immune to non-magical weapons. The kid killed the general and the wraiths vanished. Simple as that. He aimed squarely for the guts.

***

Now, 17 years later, we are still friends. I play football with him every Monday. We play RPG games, we discuss games, we are good friends.

Tom too is still a friend. In the meantime Tom has won 'a few' tournaments. He was European Champion in *L5R CCG*. Twice. And European Champion in Vampire CCG too. Not to mention becoming Polish Champion a few years in a row in both games. He wins every competition he takes part in. Fair play? Not really. Exploiting holes in the rules? Oh yes!

As you can imagine, both of these guys were my testers at some point. Why? Because they are the best players I have met in my life. If my game has a winning strategy, they will find it and point it out.

I have Martin on my team too. He is the guy who won our local Board Games League three times in a row - beating all those nerds who love *Brass, Agricola, Le Havre...*

Michal Oracz goes to tournaments of *Neuroshima Hex* and looks for the best players. If he sees a very good player, he adds him to his very own *Neuroshima Hex* team – a group of the best players in Poland. They help Michal test new armies.

***

That's how it works. That's what you need if you design games. You don't have to be a smart ass. Actually, you just need to know one.

***

I know there is a smartass out there who will beat my team one day. I know it is coming. I will read on BGG that someone found a winning strategy in one of my games. And I will cry.

But you guys have to do your best to find it. Because my team found most of these strategies before I published the game. And if there is a hole in one of my games, it is hidden in the depths of the game, hidden really really well.

I challenge you. Beat my team. Find a hole.

ABOUT TESTING GAMES, PART IV

It is late July 2009. *Stronghold* is ready. I have scheduled a few more test games to test icons and overall functionality of the board, but basically I am close to finishing this project.

It is Saturday night. We are at my friend's house and I ask them to play the *Stronghold* prototype. I set up the game, Bogas is the defender, Salou is the attacker. I watch.

We are in the first phase of the first round when something happens. Something I was not prepared for. Something I was not expecting.

Salou looks at the cards with actions. Then he looks at me and says: 'I don't like these icons. I don't get them. Screw them,' and he takes all his cards and throws them away. 'I will play only the Dispatch action today,' he says.

'What?!' I am more than in shock. 'What are you going to do? Dispatch only?!'

'I am not going to build machines, I am not going to train people, I am not going to use spells. I will just march towards the walls,' he says and begins to play.

Less than 30 minutes later he enters the castle and wins the game with a smile on his face. 'Have I just found a winning strategy?' he asks.

'You have got to be f'ing kidding me,' I say. 'You guys play again,' I order.

***

As a side note – Bogas, the player who had been defending the castle, was one of my best testers, one of the best players in my gaming group. I was devastated. Bogas was pissed off. He was doing his best, and yet, Salou's army just marched right into the castle...

***

So we play again. Salou is attacking, using no other actions than Dispatch. Bogas is defending. I help him. In fact, we work together to stop this bloody army.

In the next 40 minutes we do our utmost, but we fail. Salou wins again. He is thrilled.

I take my prototype and go home. I don't sleep. I correct the game. The next day I play again with Salou. I lose again. I tweak the prototype again. And again. And again.

Finally it is fixed. Just a few weeks before the game goes to print...

***

This story is a great example of the fourth type of testers and testing. The crazy ones. The ones who do the most ridiculous things. Who do something stupid, and yet, are able to shake up the game.

My best tester in this category is Michał Oracz. He tests the most unbelievable ways of playing the game. He looks not for straightforward strategies. He looks for holes in my system. And he is damn good at this.

We designers and publishers need a few crazy ones among our testers. If we don't have those, we will read on BGG about a tiny hole in the game that lets you earn 100 points with the blink of an eye...

***

These are the four types of testers I have. These are the four phases of testing I do. I hope you enjoyed this mini-series and that it showed you that testing games is not just sitting down with friends and playing for fun. This is work, this is very organized work, with different phases, with managing people and different goals during different phases of the process.

Keep testing games. This is damn important.

Stretch goals content

Stretch goals content

STRETCH GOALS CONTENT

STRETCH GOALS CONTENT

KICK STARTER .COM

STRETCH GOALS CONTENT

STRETCH GOALS CONTENT

Tony Boydell

Tony Boydell

TONY BOYDELL

TONY BOYDELL

TONY BOYDELL

Tony Boydell

TONY BOYDELL

Ignacy about Anythony:

Tony pisses me off. I am serious. How the hell is he able to write a new interesting post every single day. How is that even possible?! I am trying to come up with one post per week and I don't even always succeed. And Tony? I visit BGG site every day and there it is – a new post on his blog ,Every Man Needs A Shed'.

Damn you, Tony!

Besides pissing me off, he also runs a gaming company (Surprised Stare Games) and he designs great games (with Snowdonia being his most renowned board game so far). We meet each Essen, we say ,Hi' and that's it until the next year. It's brutal how game shows let us meet many great people from the industry and at the same time steal our time and don't give us a chance to talk more and get to know each other better. This last Essen we had chance to talk for a longer time – that would be 15 minutes! - because we were smart enough to schedule a meeting. Yeah, shows are that crazy...

I am happy to have Tony on board, I strongly encourage you to check out his blog at BGG and his great games!

 Follow him on twitter: @tonyboydell

MEETING ONE'S HEROES

by Anythony Boydell

It is said that you should *never meet your heroes* and, indeed, if you spend some moments Googling that phrase, you will discover many tales of expectation versus disappointment. Being an obsessive collector, and geek, my heroes are legion, and I'm lucky enough to bump into rather a lot of them whenever I travel to Essen Spiel. However, a couple of years ago I got the chance to meet someone extremely special to me...and it was 'for work'.

When I cast my mind back to memories of childhood – to the time when being a teenager was a distant aspiration, when school days ended with The Lord's Prayer - then the days are marked by the Yin/Yang of playing outside from dawn to dusk and staring, transfixed, at the television screen. Growing up in the United Kingdom in the 1970s and 1980s, there were three broadcast channels to choose from and no ubiquitous recordable/replayable media (unless you had a friend or relative with a cine projector). Children's television output was a Treasure Chest of comedy, surrealism, drama and melancholy. In particular, key programmes come in to focus from the dusty rooms of my brain: *Mr Benn, Screen Test, The Herbs, Why Don't You?, Trumpton,*

Crystal Tipps and Alistair, Hector's House, Roobarb (and Custard), The Wombles, Paddington, Noah and Nelly, Doctor Who, Play Away, Hergé's Adventures of Tintin and U.S. imports such as *Star Trek: The Animated Series, The Banana Splits Show, Planet of the Apes* and *The Six Million Dollar Man1[1]*. However, amidst this optic and sonic avalanche, the output of one production company, Smallfilms (Peter Firmin and Oliver Postgate), shines and sparkles like dew upon my soul: *The Clangers* (pink pig-mice on a remote moon), *Noggin the Nog* (Viking saga inspired by the Lewis chessmen), *Bagpuss* (toys come alive, temporarily, to mend broken things) and *Ivor the Engine*. It's hard to sufficiently express the depth of love and loyalty that these varied characters and their eclectic stories stir in me, and in many of my generation. They are nostalgic, beautifully-realized, practical, witty, subversive and utterly charming - warm-in-the-sunshine, glass-of-milk-and-a-biscuit, curled-up-on-the-sofa-with-your-favorite-toy charming.

Ivor the Engine, in particular, has never been far from my thoughts: Ivor is a railway engine who lives and works on a fictional, rural line in the top left-hand corner of Wales. He runs errands between towns such as Llangubbin, Tewyn and Llanmad ("damn all" backwards in homage to Dylan Thomas' Llareggub from *Under Milk Wood*) and has adventures along the way. Actually, I say 'adventures', but they are more a series of gentle encounters with occasional mild peril.

Ivor made a first, covert, appearance in *Paperclip Railways* (2011) – my first published foray into the train game genre – and followed, a year later, as a train in my 'breakthrough' design: *Snowdonia*. I was working in London at the time and popped into the offices of Coolabi (the media group that handles all of the Smallfilms licensing) to see whether I could use Ivor's image on a promo card. I felt so thrilled that a piece of my own invention was going to be linked, however obliquely, with the work of a childhood hero. Coolabi were welcoming and enthusiastic, and I asked - on a whim - if it might be possible to go one step further from a promo card and get a license for a full *Ivor the Engine* game?

---

[1] The Internet is your very good friend if you're interested in learning more about these gems!

"No reason why not", they said; "Just get back to us when you have something ready".

In early 2013 my thoughts turned, again, to Ivor, and what game I should design having been handed this half-a-chance. My first prototype was a ridiculous, overwrought "dumbing-down" of *Snowdonia*: worker placement with sheep and cups of tea, component-heavy and far too complex for a family market. Those beloved stories were being crushed under the weight of a graceless Eurogame, and our local gaming group were, justifiably, scornful of the mess. After I'd stopped sulking, I watched the three-hour DVD of the complete *Ivor the Engine* TV series and immersed myself in its simple pleasures: the gentle jeopardy of a spoiled hat or a motherless lamb, a lost elephant, choir practice, and the magical, yet perfectly-ordinary to the Welsh, emergence of dragons. Being a Proper Game Designer™, I also scribbled copious notes while it puffed along in front of me -linking key events and characters to the geography of the Top Left-Hand Corner of Wales. I mocked up some sample cards using library art, drafted an embryonic board layout and wrote a company biography (of Surprised Stare Games) into a presentation for Coolabi. Within a couple of weeks I received a response:

"Do you want us to talk to Peter[2], or would you like to show him the prototype yourself?"

Fast forward to July: outside it was hot; well, hot for the UK at least, with my helpful in-car computer pronouncing thirty one degrees (Celsius). I had driven for almost three hours - to meet a bona-fide hero and discuss business - and reached my destination "just outside Canterbury" at 11AM, pulling up into a square courtyard walled by a barn, a house and a cow-shed. I ding-a-linged the bell - all of the doors and windows were open to the heat - and Peter's wife, Joan Firmin, greeted me with a smile, then called out to her husband that I had arrived. Peter was in the dining room, visible from the doorstep through French windows, sat with his back to me at the table. He rose, turned

---

2 Peter Firmin - the only-surviving Smallfilms partner - –he drew and painted and hand-made all of the images and props.

and stepped onto the patio with a grin, and for the first time the reality of the situation hit me: this genial octogenarian, now shaking my shaking hand, was the man responsible for me taking up cartooning, and the man who had created the bedtime stories I had read (and am still reading) to my children. I was not a little trepidatious.

Being British, we talked – naturally - of the wonderful weather, put in an order for tea, and then I got the first part of a guided tour: the house and outbuildings had been <u>the</u> Firmin family home for more than fifty years and the place where those beloved series had been filmed. Peter may have been officially retired, but his studio was stacked with paper scraps, cuttings, layouts, sketches, lino prints, vinyl prints, frames and – teasingly – some wonderful works-in-progress. Craft knives, paint, balsa wood, model aeroplanes and papier mâché masks, book samples, proofs and pencil shavings. We returned to the dining room where Peter had been distracted, prior to my arrival, by a box of *Pippin*[3] magazine cuttings. Hundreds of pages of rare *Ivor the Engine* strips. The board game design makes use of a comprehensive library of stock images, but they only covered about two-thirds of my needs, so Peter suggested he could fill in the gaps with **new** pictures, using these magazines to remind him; this was a fantastic development! With tea and biscuits newly-delivered, I set the game prototype up and talked Peter and Joan through the mechanisms – not going into too much detail because they both admitted to being *"not very good with games"*. They were pleased with the respectful treatment of Ivor and the relative simplicity of the design and their Blessing was duly given. Joan nipped off to the kitchen to serve lunch, leaving Peter and me to amble around the lush cottage garden and chat some more: here was an Acacia tree, forty feet high or more, grown from a seed pod brought back from Zimbabwe; there stood an Oak, grown from an acorn planted by their eldest daughter. He showed me a field at the back — gone to wildflowers — now high and uncuttable with just his little push-along mower.

Lunch was pork chops, freshly-dug new potatoes and salad fresh from the vegetable patch served on a weather-beaten iron table. The shade, and the homemade Elderflower cordial, kept the three of us cool in the hazy-baking afternoon.

3 A UK children's comic, published between 1966 and 1986

A good walk after eating aids the digestion, so Peter showed me the famous barn where all of Smallfilms' labours were undertaken: *"That's where Oliver had the camera set up"*, *"here was the Clangers' moon"*, *"that's the track that allowed us to move the scenery tables around"*, and more. Our time together was drawing to a close, however, as Joan took their little terrier for a walk around the meadow. Too soon it was waves farewell. The car's air-conditioner roared in protest against the stifling heat as I crunched along the gravel drive to the main road and headed home.

(later)

Thanks to Peter's offer of new art I had to make a return visit that Winter. Mr. Firmin shuffled to the door and beamed me a straggled-bearded smile and offered a crumpled-paper handshake. *"Come in"*, he said; *"Joan is off with the dogs down the field."* On the kitchen table were some *Bagpuss*[4] paraphernalia — great boxes of First Day Covers waiting for signing because the following year (2014) would be this character's fortieth birthday. There were so many of the bloomin' things waiting for autographs that Peter had split the job between himself and his youngest daughter — the famous "Emily" of the story, a little girl who finds lost things and delivers them to the saggy old cloth cat for repair.

We retired to the lounge amongst samples of his children's crafting output and a continuous background noise of licensed goods which had been sent over "for the archives": there were books, videos, toys and miniature figures peeping from beside and behind the family photos and the furniture. All at once there was a scampering, book-ended by the opening and closing of a latched door, and two dogs trotted in, happily panting, to join us. Tim was the little one, the other – a greyhound I think - was a guest, and they leaped onto the sofa, turned exactly three times in a clockwise circle and flumped themselves down. I love dogs and I love old "family dogs" in particular: gentle, funny and loyal. Tim, a Terrier, plays the piano: Peter trained him to jump

---

4 Perhaps the most famous of Smallfilms' catalogue, Bagpuss has been voted the Nation's Favourite Children's Programme multiple times.

up on the stool and bash at the ivory with his front paws. Joan shook my one hand with her chilly two: *"Gosh, you're warm!"* she said, then toddled off to the kitchen for some cake and tea. We talked about how the Ivor the Engine game project was progressing, then Peter hopped up and fetched a flat, brown paper-wrapped parcel. These were the new pictures: a map for the board (oh, goodness) and miniature scenes for the cards. They were (and are) truly sublime and one example was a dream come true:

The Boydell family is part of Ivor's world!

Dabbing at the chocolate crumbs on my saucer, it was time to bear this precious cargo home. I haven't had another reason to meet with Peter and Joan since, but twice is two times more than I would ever have expected as a child. My experience of bringing **Ivor the Engine** to board game life has been especially special. So, don't believe the hype: you should <u>MOST DEFINITELY</u> meet your heroes!

Cédrick
Chaboussit

Cédric Chaboussit

CÉDRIC
ABOUSSIT

CÉDRIC
CHABOUSSIT

CÉDRIC CHABOUSSIT

Cédric
Chaboussit

CÉDRIC
CHABOUSSIT

Ignacy about Cédrick:

Cedric designed the best game of 2013. Period. It is called Lewis & Clark and it is a master piece. An absolute gem. One of the best games I have in my house.

And of course I have a story for you about Cedric. It was Gen con 2015. Cedric approached the Portal Games booth with Fabien and Hicham from Matagot. They talked for a couple of minutes with my wife Merry and then said ‚Goodbye' because they had to go back to work. Merry greeted Fabien and Hicham and then turned to Cedric and said: ‚It was nice to meet you. BTW: Who are you?'

‚I am Cedrick Chaboussit.' politely answered Cedric. Unfortunately, it didn't ring a bell for Merry. ‚I designed Lewis and Clark' he added very silently in a ‚sorry' tone after an awkward few seconds of silence.

Oh, yeah. That did ring a bell. Lewis and Clark is also one of Merry's most beloved game ever.

Cedric is an amazing designer. And Merry? Well, she is not only mocking me on daily basis. She also mocked the designer of Lewis and Clark! #achievementunlocked

THREE LESSONS LEARNED BY A NEWCOMER

by Cédrick Chaboussit

First of all, I would like to thank Ignacy for leaving me some space in his second book. Honestly, I'm honored to be able to express myself among such brilliant people.

As I have discovered the board gaming world from the inside recently, I would like to share with any aspiring game designers the lessons I learned from this short and intense experience as a French newcomer.

As a gamer I've always been analyzing the games I play to understand why I like some and dislike others. So naturally, I tried to design games to achieve a deeper understanding, and I quickly realized how hard it is to design a game that starts with an idea. In 2010, when I got too old to practice basketball in competition, designing games started to take up a big part of my spare time and my designs got more enjoyable.

Lesson 1: Play your games with the public at conventions

After having some prototypes tested by family and friends, I decided that the next step would be to participate in a game design competition. There is one each year in Parthenay, which is near my home, during FLIP, a summer board gaming convention. I applied both in 2011 and 2012 and was selected among the finalists, who were allotted a table for three days to show off their prototypes to the public and the jury. This was a great experience, mainly because I could see (and experience) the reactions of the public playing my games. It was intense and I could even adjust my prototypes overnight, allowing me to immediately playtest my corrections. Needless to say I learned a lot from this.

Some of the games presented at the convention ultimately got published, but this was not the case with my games. Neither did I win the competition, or find an interested publisher. This experience was an important first step, though, as I could watch people I didn't know play my games, which is quite scary when you first think about it...

I am now convinced that presenting your games at conventions is the best way to *polish* your games and eventually find a publisher (especially if he is from Poland... pun intended). With the current growth of the gaming market, there are plenty of conventions, but showing your games to the public is not sufficient.

Lesson 2: Get in touch with the right publisher in real life

Finding the right publisher is perhaps the toughest part because you need to know the publishers very well: who they are, their game range, what they are looking for, who is the boss. This information is tremendously hard to get when you first start designing games, and just browsing the Internet is definitely not enough.

The best way to get this information is to visit the big conventions and meet publishers face to face, if at all possible, which is not that easy. You have to choose the right moments, as the publishers are often busy at conventions. But there are other people who can share this information, such as other designers, agents, or bloggers. And you have to keep in mind that small publishers are easier to talk to and can grow if the market allows for it.

These two initial steps can really be time-consuming. Luckily for me, this did not turn out to be true when back in May 2012 in Toulouse I was lucky enough to have Ludonaute sitting at my table to play my prototype called *Le Village* 1900 (which later became *Lewis & Clark*). This despite the fact that we did not know each other and that they weren't really interested in playing it due to how it looked.

Ultimately, it turned out to be the best publisher for my prototype. How was this possible? Well, in fact, it wasn't as simple as it might have made it sound: a friend asked me to bring him back one of Ludonaute's prototypes for a review he was about to write in *Plato Magazine*. Anne-Cécile and Cédric kindly proposed to play my game to thank me and to give me some useful advice in return!

The two main things I learned from this experience are that:

- You should go to the big conventions and meet the publishers. If you are lucky enough, you might end up finding the right publisher for your game, i.e. people with the same vision of the final product, complementary to your skills, with whom you get on well.

- It's far better to have an attractive prototype that is visually and/or thematically strong, even if it requires a big effort from you (and I can assure you I've been there…).

Lesson 3: Be inspired!

After the successful release of *Lewis and Clark*, it naturally became easier for me to meet publishers and get to know them, which is a big plus. The game industry is a small world, with mostly nice and passionate people, which is fantastic. I now have the chance to be able to show my prototypes to the right people directly, but also meet my favorite game designers at conventions and have a chat with them!

Later, I learned that each designer starts from scratch again, regardless of what he has done before. Experience is important, but you need something special to stand out from the numerous propositions a publisher receives. No publisher will decide to publish a game if he is not convinced by the game, whoever its designer is. The publisher puts money on the table and takes the risk, and we should not forget that.

In June 2014, I had the chance to pitch another idea using the *Lewis & Clark* theme, and happily it convinced Ludonaute pretty much immediately! The game is based on an original dice flow, and it worked fine from the very beginning. It was once again developed together with Ludonaute – a wonderful cooperation. *Discoveries: The Journals of Lewis & Clark* will be released at GenCon 2015, after an unexpected prerelease in Poland. I hope for our friendship that Ignacy was not involved in this...

The most important thing needed for *Discoveries* was inspiration. Its development was more of a technical matter. That is why I also believe that each gamer is a potential designer. Gamers are critical of the games they play, as we can see by reading the detailed comments on BGG. Inspired gamers can bring fresh and successful ideas to the table, just like I did.

To conclude, this second game showed me the permanent need for inspiration in game design. Unfortunately, however, inspiration is elusive and untamable; I hope one day soon it will return to me again!

Eric
Lang

Eric Lang

ERIC
LANG

ERIC LANG

ERIC LANG

Eric
Lang

ERIC
LANG

Ignacy about Eric:

He is the best.

Ignacy about Eric again:

You want a story, huh? OK, I have one. But before we start let me put it very clear – I am a huge fan of Eric's work. I think he and Richard Garfield are two of the best game designers on this planet. Period.

So the story takes place in Dallas, at BGGcon 2014. I've just finished recording of The Dice Tower live, I am leaving the room with bunch of other people. By accident I happen to walk just next to His Majesty, Eric Lang himself. Never before have I met him in person, so this is a super cool moment for a fanboy like me. Eric turns to me and says: ‚I love your games.' I look behind me to see who is he talking to. Unfortunately, there is no designer behind me. He is clearly talking to me. What an embarrassing moment. My idol, my icon just confused me with some other designer! In a split second I am devastated. I feel really awful. In the meantime, Eric finishes his sentence. ‚Robinson Crusoe is a brilliant design.'

Then I faint. Well, almost.

He is kind. He talks a lot. He knows food. He knows pinball. He designs amazing games. He is the best.

 Follow him on twitter: @eric_lang

THE END

A STORY ABOUT BLOOD RAGE, DRAMA AND CONCLUSION

by Eric M. Lang

"Who is your character, and what do they want?"

Syd Field, author of *Screenplay*, poses this as the first question to a writer beginning work on their screenplay. As advice goes, it's concise, logical and obvious in hindsight. It's a pretty good start when you're writing any story in any medium. Stories are compelling because they are told from a point of view, and it makes sense that this is the first thing both the writer and reader want to understand.

Mr. Field posits that the writer needs to know the answer to these two questions intimately, and the reader should know them within the first five minutes of the film. Clarity. Focus. Velocity.

Games don't deliver stories in the same way as other media, but you can bet your last dollar they do tell stories. Every last one of them.

As a medium, stories' point of view is through characters. People. It's how we relate. What is the point of view in a game? The players, clearly. So Mr. Field's lesson crosses mediums quite well here.

Who is your character, and what do they want? Alright, let's start there.

Except I didn't start there, and that's why I always get in trouble.

Glorious Failure

I love stories and have been writing stories since I could pick up a pencil. In junior high school and early adulthood I wrote full novels in almost every science fiction and fantasy genre I enjoyed reading. I fancied myself a writer; still do to a degree.

The best stories I wrote had clarity of vision and focus. I knew who my character was and what they wanted. Framing it in this way was not always conscious to me, but in retrospect it's abundantly clear. The rest fell into place, and the parts that didn't were those that did not align with those central questions.

When I started working on *Blood Rage*, I knew I wanted a big box game of pillaging Viking clans jam-packed with strategy and aggression.

What I didn't know or understand enough at the beginning was who the players were, and *what they want*. I knew "points" were the victory condition; I understood that "points" were a good mechanical way to aggregate a number of threaded and overlapping strategies, but I didn't quite grok the "why." It seems like such a subtle distinction, but the lack of this knowledge was the source of much dissonance early on.

After the first two months of design, I had a strong and cohesive set of mechanics in a play space with tons of strategic possibility.

What I lacked was clear and focused immersion, and because of that I almost threw the entire game away.

Clarity

Blood Rage is a game about Viking clans pillaging the remains of the land during Ragnarök, the end of the world. It's got a board, gorgeous miniatures of Vikings, dragonships and monsters, card drafting, victory points, and oodles of strategy.

Sounds cool, doesn't it? As a game player, the above probably excites your imagination. It delivers the vague promise of thematic possibilities. Hearing that makes me want to pick up the box and paw through the components.

But it doesn't imply game play. It doesn't stem from a point of view.

I woke up one night after a bad playtest. (My testers had liked the game well enough, but they didn't spend time telling each other stories afterwards, which for *Blood Rage* was a point of failure to me.) I ran to my desk and typed these words:

"I am a Chieftain of Clan Bear. I was released from Valhalla to prove to the gods my might, piety and battle prowess. Because at the end of the world, Glory is all."

Not as refined as the final vision statement, but it was a start. I had discovered my point of view. I had discovered what the victory condition needed to be *about*, and *why*.

Focus

With renewed vigor, I started removing strategic depth from the game. I cut at least half of the strategic possibilities, which to many would seem a crime, but it was freeing, lifting the scales from my eyes.

Every path to Glory had to be explainable from the point of view of impressing the gods at the end of the world. Player's might is defined by the levels achieved in their three Clan Stats (the final two levels of which give major Glory awards). It is gained by pillaging. Players' piety is defined by the quests given by the gods and by dying in the provinces doomed by Ragnarök. Battle prowess is earned by killing opponents in battle. All other actions need to supplement those three primary foci.

Battle in *Blood Rage* is not the result of one player attacking another; it is the byproduct of the Viking Clans showing off to the gods. When one player pillages, others may join in to stop them with the intent to destroy them (impressing Thor and Odin), lose and slyly make it cost more to the enemy (impressing Loki), or overpower them with battle tactics (impressing Tyr).

This set up a dynamic where players felt like they *needed* to be a part of as many battles as possible; like they were missing out on Glory if they sat out.

I removed all "area control" mechanical arcs from the game, save those reserved for hidden quests. In early versions of the game, players gained Glory for every province they controlled. But it seemed so mundane, impious. Why did the gods care about this, unless it was on a quest given *specifically to a Clan?*

Velocity

The best games have victory conditions that imply game play and even some strategy. But most importantly, they provide clear velocity. When the "how" of your actions (understanding the mechanical hoops through which games make you jump to meet milestones) align with the "why" (how these milestones add up to victory), players are more likely to achieve flow.

And while in that perfect state of flow - where challenge and reward are perfectly balanced - players are free to narrate their way through the game. The story becomes clearer, and (hopefully) more compelling.

The Glorious Conclusion

"Who am I and what do I want?" is the narrative translation for "how do I win?" The primary take away for me during the process of the design of *Blood Rage* was that I needed a better contextual understanding of the game's desired ending before I could begin. Clear understanding of "who are we and what do we want?" instinctually drives narrative forward, and the rest of the game design is about throwing obstacles in that path (the challenge).

And because games are navigated by players who (usually) provide their own opposition and drama, the burden of understanding the causal relationship between mechanics, action and victory needs to be as low as possible.

As a designer, my victory condition is to elevate, challenge and transport players during their time with me, while easing their burden.

That is my character, and that's what I want.

Ignacy, thank you dearly for the opportunity to explore game design space from this point of view.

Bruno
Faidutti

Bruno Faidutti

BRUNO
FAIDUTTI

Bruno
Faidutti

BRUNO
FAIDUTTI

Ignacy about Bruno:

It was 2007. We were one of the most popular and successful game companies in Poland. And of course, no one outside Poland has ever heard of us. We were planning our first Essen show. Damn you, Tony!

Actually I don't remember how, but somehow I managed to get information that Bruno will visit Poland that summer. I contacted him and asked if it is possible to meet. He agreed. We played games, we talked about games, it was a great time.

Later that summer, Bruno published a review of Neuroshima Hex. Along with the Polish Game of the Year award we received, and two more reviews, it was all we had to create a buzz for the game for Essen. We succeeded. His review, his recommendation, was a huge help for us. The international career of Portal Games began.

With no doubt, Portal would not be in a place where we are today without Bruno. He was kind and happy to help from the first time we met. He might not know it, but this is true – his name is written on the founding stone of Portal Games and will be there forever.

BTW: he designs amazing games. But you knew that already, huh?

 Follow him at his website: www.faidutti.com/blog/

WHAT STORIES DO BOARD GAMES TELL?

by Bruno Faidutti

So, board games tell stories. Ignacy coined the phrase, but the idea is not new, and I have been pushing it almost since I started designing board games in the early eighties. As a game designer, I've always felt like a very lazy novelist, designing the backbone and general structure of the story, and stopping just when the hard work - meaning the actual writing - should have started. This means both that board games indeed tell stories, and that they don't tell them in the same way as books, or movies, or even role playing games. Neither do they tell the same stories every time, and, in a way, always tell two different but interwoven stories.

A game doesn't need zombies, astronauts or Russian gnome submariners to tell a story. Even the most abstract games are story builders, as can be seen with chess. A game of chess has no setting, it's not really a representation of war, but it has a beginning and an end, it has suspense and reversals, and it can be dramatically retold - so every game is a different story. Of course, this is even more true of a game of *Zombicide*.

There is, however, an important difference between games on the one hand, and movies, or novels, or even music on the other. The game itself is not a story, it's a story generator. The game designer didn't really write the story, he built an engine that is later used by the players to build their own stories - and that's where the laziness is.

Games and toys are, in theory, completely different things. A game has strict rules, and must be played accordingly, while a toy has no fixed rules, and can be played with freely. Most people, however, consider games and toys to be very similar things, and the same verb, to play, is used to describe the activity of using one or the other (it's also used for a theater play, which could lead to more interesting developments). The reason for this is probably that we feel intuitively that every game is something like a book, but it's also more or less a toy. It's not completely one, because the players cannot do what they want with it, but it's far more of a toy than a book or a movie, because the story it tells depends on the players, and isn't always the same.

Gaming is both about freedom and constraints - it's about making free decisions under strictly constraining rules, while real life is about making decisions of which we don't know if they are really free, under extremely mysterious rules. The reader of a book, or the watcher of a movie, can make very few free decisions. He can have his own interpretation of what is happening in the story, he can move faster or slower (unless he's watching a movie at a theater), he can quit, but he cannot change a word in the text. A book or a movie tells a story, but it's always telling more or less the same story. A game tells a different story each time you play it - even when these stories have lots in common. That's why playing the same game again and again is much more common, more justifiable, more interesting, and more exhilarating than reading the same book again and again.

Video gamers, or role playing gamers, could reproach me for ignoring the recent trend towards narratives. It's true that video games and role playing games are more and more often built like novels, with a very directive scenario in which the players' actions are mostly a means to express their personality without much effect on the storyline. Something similar to this can also be found in board games, mostly in cooperative games, but it's only marginal and, even in the most directive cooperative games, such as *Pandemic*, the story doesn't really feel scripted.

Like books or movies, games can be short or long, light or heavy, simple or complex. But the genres, and the emotions they generate, are not the same. There are lots of romantic books and movies, and specifically lots about love stories, but no romantic game - and the idea of designing one does not sound that exciting to me. One of the reasons is that a player doesn't always embody a character - he can embody a city, a nation, a company, an alien race, and sometimes very vague and abstract entities. Another and more interesting reason might be that, paradoxically, the fact that players can influence the storyline and the outcome of the game results in a far less empathic relation with the characters, because the players are not really 'carried away' by the story, engulfed in fate. We can't really believe in a story that we can actually control, and the temporary suspension of disbelief in a game is much more superficial than in a book or movie. It is comparable to looking at a painting, which also doesn't let us get carried us away by the story, and for which we have to imagine, and therefore control, the past and future. As a result, where many people often weep when reading a book or watching a movie, no player that I know has ever wept after losing a game. This is even true of role playing games, in which even the death of one's decade old character never feels as dramatic as the death of Emma Bovary or Anna Karenina. Games can be terribly tense, but they are never really sad - the only board game that I know which manages to convey a real and overwhelming feeling of fate and sadness is *The Grizzled (Les Poilus)*, an antimilitarist card game about life in the trenches during the first world war - after playing it, one feels similar to how one feels after reading *All Quiet on the Western Front*.

There's no romance in games, but there's competition - even in so-called cooperative games, which are in fact about fighting together against a common enemy. This explains why there are so many war or even race games, war and race being the epitomizations of the two main types of human conflict, fighting one against the other or competing for a prize. There are some novels and movies about war, but not that many, and usually they include a desperate love story or a story of (male) friendship and bonding. There are very few race movies, and personally I have not heard of a single race novel. As for building trail networks or developing a city, these don't sound like very exciting storylines for a book or movie, unless there is an underlying story of love, crime or vengeance added.

As an interesting aside, there's a genre that is as popular in books, movies and games: deduction and detective stories. The reason is probably that whodunit books or movies are more similar to games than any other literary genre. The reader of a crime story, at least if the story is good and the reader likes the genre, is not 'carried away' by the novel as he would potentially be by a romance or adventure novel. He is investigating, he is trying not only to guess, but actually to find out what will happen. This is not exactly playing a game, but it's more akin with playing than brooding about a sad romance.

Games are highly interactive, while novels and books are not. Players must build the story, and must always think in tactical or strategic terms, aiming for victory. This leaves little room for subtle feelings, for romance, for empathy. The story told by a game can be complex and intricate, but its setting has to remain simple, obvious, and be entirely mastered by the players before the game even starts. That is why the action of so many games take place in very simplistic exotic settings, be they orientalist, historic, Western, or Martian. I won't go into details here since I've already written a very long article on this topic on my blog (http://faidutti.com/blog/?p=3780). There is less text, and less depth in a game than in a movie, like there's less text and less depth in a movie than in a novel. Furthermore, during a game, gamers spend most of their intellectual energy trying to make the best of the rules in order to find a winning strategy - the theme must help them, must make the game elements easier to analyze, so it doesn't really matter if it's true or simplistic as long as it's easy to grasp. This can also be the case in novels and movies, but it's often the reverse, the storyline being a tool used to lure the reader into the depth and truth of the world described. In the best books and movies it goes both ways. This is because, with most books and movies, one doesn't spend much time and energy asking oneself how to read, how to watch - one just reads or watches. With games, most of the time is spent thinking of tactics, of strategy, of opponents' psychology, which leaves little time and brain power for dealing in depth with a serious topic. That is also why games can't be very political, or only in a very simple and demonstrative way, never in a reflexive one.

Paradoxically, while the story told by a game is not entirely written before the game is played, it doesn't necessarily leave more room for the player's imagination - or at least for thematic imagination. As I have said before, a board game player is usually more engaged in a strategic reflection than in romantic reverie, and while the story is incomplete, the setting is more squared and limited than in a book or novel. The reader of a novel is usually trying to 'understand' it, to find out how the characters think and act, and therefore what is driving the story. There is always something more than what is openly written or told, because the author of the novel, or the movie scenarist, had a precise idea of his characters' motives and drives. These motives and drives are easier to understand in some novels and movies than in others, but they are never expressed as clearly as in a game rule.

The ruleset is the only text in a game, but the rules are not a story - they are a tool used by the players to write the story. Therefore, what drives the story is clearly and openly disclosed in a game, whereas it is more or less hidden in a book or novel. A game's story can't have the same 'hidden depth' as a novel or movie.

Of course, the interactive decisions of the players are also important, and can add some element of human mystery to the game's story, at least if they don't rely on purely deterministic calculations. Great chess players will tell you that every good player has a style, which means there is something human and deeper than abstract strategy in the game - and this is even more true of poker and all games that rely a great deal on players' psychology. I don't think, however, one will ever find, or even just look for, the same psychological intricacies in explaining his opponent's moves at chess or poker than in explaining Emma Bovary's, or even Jane Eyre's, thoughts and decisions.

When reading what I have written so far, I notice there is a striking ambiguity in what I call a game's story. Sometimes, it is the thematic story unfolded by the game's rules and the players' actions, such as, for example, the story of survivors of a shipwreck on a deserted island. Sometimes, it is the story of the relationships between the players, of the conservative play of this player versus the risky moves of another, and of the tension that builds up between them. Both stories are interrelated, the former is in part the result of the latter, and the latter can inform the former if a player tries to act out the part of their character. One could say it's the same with movies, but unless you're a professional actor, you would probably consider the story of a movie to be the story told in the movie, not the story of what happened between the actors when they staged it, a story, what's more, that the spectator usually doesn't even know. In a game, these two stories are more or less intertwined, and this might be what makes the stories told by games so endearing.

I like games that tell compelling stories, and that tell stories in both senses. It's probably why I like to design games in which players cannot hide themselves behind the rules, behind the cards, behind their pawns - games that are actually played with and against the other players and not with and against cardboard components. It's also probably why I like games with a clear and strong thematic storyline, which usually means a very caricatural story. If a game gives you both a strong theme in which to build the story, and incentives for players to build it together, usually meaning player against player, it's a good game.

Ludovic
Maublanc

Ludovic Maublanc

LUDOVIC
AUBLANC

LUDOVIC MAUBLANC

Ludovic
Maublanc

LUDOVIC
MAUBLANC

Ignacy about Ludovic:

It was summer 2006 when I decided I'll try to explain to Merry what I do for living. I invited her to a board games event to present her a couple of games.

Of course, I choose Settlers of Catan. And to my surprise, she hated it. She really did hate it. After the game she said that board games are boring and it is not for her. I was devastated. It looked like this is over, she was refusing to try any other game. Board games and Merry looked like a very short story without a happy end.

And then I did something desperate – please, try one more game and if you don't like it, I'll never bother you with games again. She agreed. It looked like a cheap way to throw away board games from her life once and for all.

In this crucial moment, in this turning point of our lives, in this moment of truth... I chose Ludovic's ‚Cash'n'Guns'.

You know the rest of the story. Merry is an avid gamer. Board games are her passion. A few years later I married her.

Ludovic, thank you.

Ah, BTW: besides Cash'n'Guns, Ludovic designed a few other freaking awesome games like Mr. Jack (Merry hates it), Cleopatra (Merry hates it), Rampage (Merry hates...). Well, I was pretty lucky choosing the right Ludovic design! ;)

 Follow him on twitter: @LudovicMaublanc

STRIPPING THE UNNECESSARY

by Ludovic

In 2014, the second edition of my most popular game, *Ca$h 'n Guns* came out. But it was not simply a second edition, it was a complete reworking of the game. It is rare for an author to have the opportunity to return to one of his very first games after a few years of experience.

Ca$h 'n Guns was indeed one of my first game ideas. I was young, full of energy and I used to make two new prototypes every month! There was a lot of trash among these ideas, obviously, but from time to time, an interesting idea popped out from it all, and *Ca$h 'n Guns* was, to me, something that needed to be made.

Games inspired by gameplay are often opposed to games inspired by a theme, but for me, these two elements are not the start of an idea for a game, but tools to make this idea come to life. The first idea for *Ca$h 'n Guns* was to create a classic gangster movie scene around the table where everyone is pointing their guns at each other, staring at each other, a drop of sweat on the forehead and asking themselves if their opponent's gun is loaded.

To create this atmosphere, I needed accessories like guns, a goal like loot to share, and a bluff mechanic, in this case each player having a limited amount of shooting cards.

For the accessories, I used the gangster theme to justify the fact that players were armed. For all I know, they could have been cowboys, pirates or even magicians with magic wands. The truth is, I still really like toys and wanted some in my game.

For the loot, I used an amount of cash that we would put on the table for everyone to share. Players could threaten each other and those who didn't give up could share the loot... It would be easy, but why would these fearless gangsters give up so easily? Now I needed a gameplay mechanic.

I did not need to go and look too far. The players only had one card in each round, and only a few cards allowed you to really shoot at your opponent (Bang!). The other cards were only decoys (Click). After testing the game a few times, it seemed that 8 rounds was a good number and 3 Bangs and 5 Clicks seemed to be a good ratio. To add some diversity, I added a special effect to one of the 3 Bangs that would allow a player to shoot faster than the others.

The game was starting to take shape.

Finally, I needed one last element to keep the game overflowing with anxiety and tension, simply because I'm a sadistic person. When a player was targeted by a Bang and did not give up, he was shot... And if someone was shot at three times, they were out of the game! I don't really like elimination games, as I find it kind of sad to participate in a game, listen to the rules and be kicked out after a few minutes to see the others having fun without you. But to build up enough tension during the hold-up part, I needed a strong punishment for the players to ask themselves if it was really a good idea to stay in the game. And let's be realistic, if a player was kicked out of the game, it might have been because several players were pointing at him and he himself decided to stay in the game and take the chance... It was his own decision and neither a random event in the game, nor the will of the other players that made him lose.

All of this was the basis of the game, and fairly early on it proved to work all by itself. This was great news because I'm quite lazy as an author, even though I did make a lot of prototypes at the beginning of my "career", though this was mainly because I had a tendency to give up on a project that took too long to get it to work and would skip to the next project. I'm not really interested in adjustments. That's also why I mostly work with other authors. It's easier to motivate each other or to hand over a project to the other when you can't stand it anymore!

Ca$h 'n Guns was made by me and only me, even though its final shape owes a lot to the editors, Thomas and Cedrick, the founders of Repos Production and its only members at the time. They made numerous improvements to make this game the success it has become and still be available in stores ten years later…which is quite an achievement in this market.

Within 10 years, the game has sold out many times, and the day has come for the editor to ask himself if it would be a good idea to spruce up the game. In fact, this seems pretty logical after 10 years of service. The main idea was to give the game a makeover, but the editor asked me if I would like to use this opportunity to redo it completely. So I reinvented the game with my more experimented eyes and damn, I changed everything!

The game might be simple, but I knew that some points in the rules were still too obscure for beginners. I'm sure some players still don't get how the "fast shot" works after their first play! I introduced this element to introduce a tactical side into the game, but is it worth it when no one knows how to use it? Into the trash it went!

Some players forgot the function of some of their secret powers during the game, or they didn't use them the way they were supposed to be used. The special powers were added to give some variety to the game, to distinguish the character of a player and help him step into the game world. Therefore, if the player did not use it, we had missed the point, so I decided to replace them with visible powers.

The main question was, "What can I remove from the game without the game becoming less fun?" Actually, this is the question I ask myself every time I finalize a game. Everything that is not essential will be removed. It is useless to write a whole paragraph of rules for an obscure event that will only happen every once in a while during the game and won't add any more fun.

At the time, I probably lacked perspective to smooth things out.

Those of you who know the two editions of the game will probably tell me that the sharing part seems more complex now than before. Actually, as I said before, the sharing part was more a pretext to have guns than a real issue (remember my love for toys). Now I find it kind of sad, because in the end we only tried to eliminate the richest players or the ones we did not like. A lot of players couldn't see the point of choosing to target one player over another.

That is how the idea of the Godfather came about. The sharing process won't be fair anymore, for the Godfather now takes some money first and then the others can have their share. There is an intended imbalance between the players at the beginning of the game, and the hold-up part becomes a way to take advantage of this imbalance.

The new additions to the loot have the same purpose. With the money, there are now other things like diamonds and paintings which give you points, the general idea being the more you have, the better it is… and you don't want the others to collect what you are collecting! It gives you the ability to really choose who you will shoot. If you're collecting diamonds, you'll have to check who is collecting them too and you'll shoot him when the time comes!

It's not easy to know when a game is done. There is a moment when everything works, but you keep asking yourself if you should still change one minor detail or perhaps another. You need to know when to stop and when the creative process is over. I thought I had managed to do this 10 years ago with the first edition. Actually, there still was a lot of work to be done to achieve the atmosphere I wanted the game to have. Maybe in 10 years (if I'm still alive) I will realize I could have gone even further, and will then create a third edition ;).

Bonus tips:

- Don't depend on alliances; they will fall apart during the game.
- If four or more people are targeting you, just let it go for god's sake!
- Check on people who are collecting diamonds and paintings, even if you aren't collecting them yourself.
- Beware of the quiet ones; they always win in the end.
- Hold your gun like a gangsta; the usual way is too main stream and less frightening.
- Don't let your friend translate your article from French to English; she'll probably end up adding some rotten stuff like you being a sadist.

Mike Fitzgerald

Mike
Fitzgerald

MIKE
FITZGERALD

MIKE FITZGERALD

MIKE
FITZGERALD

Mike
Fitzgerald

MIKE
FITZGERALD

Ignacy about Mike:

It's BGGcon 2014 in Dallas. I am waiting for the elevator at ground floor. At some point I hear someone singing Why Can't We Be Friends. Mike approaches me with a huge smile on his face. Positive energy fills the whole floor.

I don't know if you guys already noticed, but I keep saying it over and over - this guy is the kindest person I know. This guy is so nice. This dude is so funny. And so on and so on.

Mike is the kindest person I know. He is nice, he is funny. Mike is the person - the moment you meet him, you immediately know he is your best friend.

Are all designers the same? Kind, polite, funny? I don't know. Most of those I know, yes.

Is that because our job? Because we build things to make people happy? Because we help people socialize, enjoy time with friends, build family bonds? I have no idea what's the thing, but there is something here, something in the air, something in this industry – smile, kindness, friendship.

I am so proud to be part of this family. And so happy that we have Mike. He is the best.

THE STORY OF A BASEBALL 'DIAMOND'

by Mike Fitzgerald

I am a lifelong Baseball fan. When I was a kid, my father would take me to Yankee and Met games and tell me all about the glory days when the Giants and Dodgers were also in New York. I started playing statistical baseball games when I was a teenager. These included **APBA** (my favorite) and *Strat-O-Matic*. They were fun simulations of games where real players would perform like they did in real life.

I am also a lifelong card game fan. As a kid I played *Rummy* and *Hearts* with my sister and cousin. We had a 1 million *Rummy* game going over several years instead of the more modest 500 *Rummy*.

Flash forward several years and I am a radio personality in New York about to leave my radio career to become a full time game designer, which I had been doing part time for many years. This got me thinking of game ideas that I had put on hold earlier because I did not have enough time to do them right.

The first thought that came to me was Baseball. I knew I did not want to do a simulation Baseball game, that type of game is well represented by many great titles. I am a big fan of *Dominion* and I thought using the deck building engine would be an interesting starting point.

I wanted the sense of building your team strategically for some kind of tactical baseball game play. All of my early versions were fun, strategically, but I had no real game to play in between buying players. We just showed our hands and the players had runs on them. Add up your runs and then see who beat who. You could play with up to 5 players and you might go 4-0, or 2-2 depending on your run count versus the other players. Many of my play testers liked this a lot, but I thought it was much too close to *Dominion*, and did not give me the feel of baseball I was looking for. I started to put some affects on the players that would alter the cards they were facing when players exposed their hands for run count. This felt a bit better, but was too fiddly and still lacked real baseball strategy. I would put the game on the shelf and come back to it every couple of months and try again.

The first big break through was when I decided to make it a 2 player game so I could bring out the real strategic struggle in a game. I started with a 9 card hand for each player and then going back and forth till all 9 cards had been played and most runs won. I felt I was on the right track, but the scores were way too similar and there still was not enough real baseball feel to it. One player was at bat while the other was in the field, and this made the game way too short, but would require a huge hand to feel like a real game.

I wanted a 5 minute mini game between each buy round so you could feel like your team was really changing during a series of games. I had no idea if this was even possible, but I knew I was not calling it done until I had achieved it. Back on the shelf it went. This was 2013.

When struggling with a game I often take breaks to play newer games and some old favorites to see if this will loosen my brain and spark some new thoughts. I played *Clubs* by North Star Games right after it came out. I liked this game a lot, as it takes the climbing game mechanism and makes it more accessible to a wider audience. I had just put the Baseball game on the shelf the night before and this made me think that now we have a Hearts, Spades and Clubs game, but what about Diamonds? Within a week I had the basic idea of what was to become *Diamonds*. I knew I wanted to make a trick taking game that was very simple and easy to learn, but offered something unique to the genre. I decided to make a Trump game with no trump.

Over the years I have noticed that many casual card game players have trouble with the concept of Trump. In many hobby trick taking games the trump rules keep changing and the games can be beyond casual players. I decided to base the actual playing of cards on *Whist*. By giving each suit a different action I could make a Trump suit without calling it that. That is how Diamonds got to have the best action in the game and players need to treat it like a Trump suit in other games. This design came together very quickly, while my work on the Baseball Diamond was moving at a much slower pace.

One night during a *Diamonds* play test we were trying to balance the actions of the suits and one player said, 'Why can't the Hearts action put 2 diamonds in your showroom instead of 1?'

Eureka moment number 1:

The only part of that sentence that I heard was "2 Diamonds" and my brain did a flip and said, 'Of course, we need 2 Diamonds for the Baseball Game so each player could have men on base at the same time.' I thanked the play tester for such a great idea for the Baseball Game, but we found it was not a good idea for *Diamonds*. From that moment on I was in full time work mode on *Baseball* and *Diamonds* at the same time.

The play testing for *Diamonds* went very well and soon the game was done and ready to be shown to publishers.

Baseball came back off the shelf and I made two Diamonds so each player had his own set of bases to work with. Now I was saying goodbye to any kind of realistic simulation of a baseball game (or so I thought). I needed a way to have each card played affect your own playing field and/or your opponent's playing field. This is where the immediate action part of a card and the Hit Box for threatened Hits started. I was so far from a simulation of baseball at this point that I created a future where this game could be simulating highlights of a game. Writing the back story for this game was really fun and allowed me to mash up names of famous baseball players from the past, since the game was set in the distant future. My oldest daughter Lauren is an excellent writer and she came up with a short story about one of the 'Natural' players in the game, which shows what it is like to have to play alongside Cyborgs and Robots. (See the story at the end of this article.) I loved this story so much that the Magna Glove became a part of the game in an expansion.

It was a little tricky for players to pick up the action/resolve/threaten parts of each turn, but once they played a game or two it seemed to come natural. The scores were too low still, but I kept at it, determined to find the answer on how to get realistic scores. I also was having trouble coming up with enough different attributes for players to make enough of them to make the deck building choices interesting.

Eureka moment number 2:

I was changing cards on the fly one day before a play test. I just cross off and mark changes directly on the cards until they are so messy I have to make a new version. I was changing a Single to a Home Run on a player's card and forgot to scratch off the Single. During the play test this card was played and I looked at it and said this guy threatens a Single and a Home Run. My tester and I both laughed at first, but then it hit me: This is how to make the scores more realistic and open up more attributes for players. A Player can have multiple hits in his Hit Box. Wow, was I excited. In two weeks I had what I thought was a really fun game. I had no idea if I could get a game company interested and I had no idea if players outside of my play test circle would like it.

Would baseball fans feel enough baseball in the game? Would casual fans find the game fun enough as a game alone to enjoy it? I had no idea.

The first game company I showed it to loved the game. However, the owner said, because it is a two player game with a sports theme he would have trouble selling the game. That is what I kept hearing until I showed it to Eagle-Gryphon Games. Sean Brown, Ralph Anderson and Rick Soued were all impressed with the game play and are all big sports fans. They were not afraid to take an unusual theme and turn it into something special. The fact that Ralph was an old and dear friend of mine and was the main person developing the game did not hurt either.

I then showed *Diamonds* to the company that turned down Baseball. This time Stephen Buonocore of Stronghold Games said it was not the usual type of game he publishes, but it is really fun and since he was starting a new Pocket Line, it would fit in nicely there.

I ended up with two games each, with the best publisher for each game. I am very proud of both of these games.

BASEBALL 2045
The Natural's Tale by Lauren Fitzgerald

All Tony McGuire wants to do is get home, pop open a nice cold can of ElectroBuzz, and relax in the massage pod. But the roaring mob outside the stadium has other plans for him.

"Tony! Over here! I'm your biggest fan!"

"I love you Tony!"

"Great game today, McGuire!"

Pushing aside the pain and fatigue, Tony grins for the cameras, shakes the outstretched hands, and signs the baseballs, slowly working his way through the crowd.

"When I grow up, I'm gonna be a Natural just like you!" shouts a little boy, and every kid within earshot calls out, "Me too!"

It takes all the self-control Tony can muster to keep himself from blurting out how nearly impossible it will be for any of these kids to make it as a Natural. Or worse, how in reality, being a Natural often feels just one step above being the team mascot. Just some guy in a costume, dancing around to make the fans happy, while the 'bots and 'borgs play baseball.

"That's great, buddy," he says. "Keep on practicing and you'll get there some day!"

It can't hurt a kid to have a dream, right? Might even help keep him out of trouble. And who knows, maybe someday, when the novelty of all this fancy technology wears off, the game will go natural again. Ha, Tony thinks. Now I'm the one dreaming.

"How's your wrist, Tony?" a fan calls out, and the sweetness of her voice almost disrupts his resolve to keep smiling. He wants to tell her, whoever she is, that at this very moment his wrist is throbbing with excruciating pain. He wants to confide that for a split second there, he almost wasn't going to try to catch that ball, because he knew how hard that 'bot had hit it, and he knew how bad it was going to hurt. But he caught it because not catching it would have earned him a one-way ticket to the Minors. With so many Naturals competing to get on teams, Tony is acutely aware of how lucky he is. How easily he could be replaced. There is no room for error or injury. Or honesty, for that matter. He finds the face belonging to the sweet voice, and immediately looks away, lest her tender expression bring out more emotion than he cares to reveal. He forces his smile to beam even brighter, and gives the crowd an enthusiastic thumbs-up, the gesture itself sending a shock of pain down his forearm.

Ned Lund, a news reporter who has built his career writing about Naturals like Tony, yells out from behind his trademark large black plastic-framed glasses (worn to protest the practice of universal eyesight correction surgery at birth), "Tony! Heard a rumor that you might be switching to the MagnaGlove! Can you confirm or deny?"

"No comment," says Tony, maintaining his smile and continuing to shake any hands in his way.

"Come on, man! You're one of the last true Natties in the game! You can't sell out now!"

Ned Lund's argument is drowned out by the noise of the 'bot cart, a fancy parade-like Float designed to showcase one of the team's robots after each game. Giant speakers blast Lava Core music, flashing red and green lights bounce off the robot's shiny exterior, and Higgins, the scrawny robot caretaker, jogs alongside the cart trying to rev up the crowd.

Tony recognizes Slammer, one of the newest and most powerful 'bots, on display today. Turned on, at the plate, Slammer is an amazing hitting machine, a force to be reckoned with, a feat of modern engineering. Turned off, propped up and posed on the 'bot cart, he is just a hunk of metal. An empty suit of armor. A huge, unwieldy collection of parts, that happens to have a poorly designed and slightly horrifying face. Tony's smile twists into a smirk momentarily as he observes the effect of the spectacle on the crowd. Many of the people who had greeted him so enthusiastically now hang back as a smaller, rowdier group emerges, fists pumping. Dressed like Lava Core singers and screaming just as loud, the 'bot fanatics chant Slammer's name over and over as Higgins rattles off technical details about the 'bot's construction in a hoarse falsetto that no one can hear.

Slammer's arrival gives Tony a chance to make his escape. A few lingering fans chant "McGuire's on FIRE!" and Ned Lund hollers one more question, something about the rivalry between Naturals and Cyborgs, but Tony just keeps on walking. He's done enough public relations for one day, he thinks. Back in the safety of his vehicle, he takes a moment to rub some Blue Freeze on his aching wrist. The relief almost brings tears to his eyes. And there, in his duffel bag, he spots the still unopened gift that his coach had given him earlier, to "recognize his significant contributions to the team." He doesn't need to open it to know what it is. But he tears the yellow paper back just enough to confirm his suspicion. The unmistakable MagnaGlove logo stares up at him. The only people with the money and connections to access the MagnaGlove are the baseball big shots, he knows. And when the baseball big shots send you a pretty package claiming to be a token of appreciation, he knows it's not a gift. It's an ultimatum.

Mike Elliot

Mike Elliot

MIKE ELLIOT

MIKE ELLIOT

Mike Elliot

MIKE ELLIOT

Ignacy about Mike:

I met Mike in Dallas, BGGcon, 2014. We were standing in a hotel lobby with a group of people, Eric Lang introduced us, we said ‚Hello' and suddenly the group split, everybody walked in different directions. I never saw Mike again.

You can't build a good story out of that, huh?

Mike designed Thunderstone. With Eric M. Lang he co-designed Quarriors! and then Dice Masters. He co-designed Shadowrun: Cross-fire. He co-designed Star Trek: Fleet captains. Big IP's, great mechanisms, and – for some reason – Mike is there, hidden in the shadow.

I needed to connect all the dots to see that there is one designer behind all those titles. I hope that his article about working on big IP's will help you connect some dots too.

And in the meantime my short term goal is super simple. Get to know Mike better! I definitely won't allow him to disappear again in the lobby.

 Follow him on twitter: @Elliott_Games

MY SUPERHERO ORIGIN STORY

by Mike Elliott

At the end of this year, I will have been a game designer for 20 years. I originally wanted to tell Ignacy the story about adapting one of my favorite IPs to a game, but the story that I tell people most frequently is the story of how I ended up in the game industry, so that's what I'll start with. While I enjoy telling the story, I do tell it a lot and I figure if I tell it here, everyone will see it, since I expect everyone I know to read Ignacy's book, and I'll be done with it once and for all.

My superhero origin story it is, then. It all started with a road trip. A friend of mine invited me to come out for the weekend to a beach house in Del Mar, California. It poured nonstop the entire weekend, so we were not able to spend any time outside at the beach. His dad was there and he taught us how to play *Bridge*. Prior to that, I had played chess and many board games and card games, but Bridge was the first game I really enjoyed for its strategic depth and balance. While *Bridge* was, and still is a game associated with an older crowd, I started playing a lot and had a group of friends around my age and we would get together and play at tournaments. We would all stay at the same hotel or house and after the sessions we would play games late into the night.

During one such event in Los Angeles in 1994, one of my friends, Jeff Goldsmith, introduced me to Magic. I thought it was a great game and I started playing a lot, to the point where my Bridge friends started getting upset that I was playing *Magic* all the time and not playing *Bridge* anymore. This was in the days before the Pro Tour and a lot of the stores would run local events, many of which were heavily attended. I was at an event at Arizona State University in 1995 and I started chatting with a couple of guys about what I thought was wrong with *Magic*. It happened that they both worked for Wizards of the Coast, and they invited me up to interview for a position, and hired me to work in R and D. So I moved up to Seattle, got splashed with some radioactive waste while pushing a guy out of the way of a truck, and developed game designer powers, which I only use for good of course.

That is the main part of my "How I got where I am today" story. I worked for 10 years at Wizards of the Coast, mostly on *Magic*. I worked on 30 expansions for *Magic* and designed over 1000 cards and many mechanics. While I was at Wizards, I worked on *Pokémon* for a while and also designed a very popular Japanese trading card game called *Duel Masters,* which is still my most successful game, even though it never got traction in the US or Europe. I left Wizards in 2005 and decided I would try freelancing for a while. I met Eric Lang at a trade show in Las Vegas and we became friends. He gave me some tips on how to talk to publishers, how to get meetings, and what conventions to attend. It was all extremely helpful. We ended up collaborating later on several games, including *Quarriors* and *Dice Masters.*

Breaking in as a freelancer was not an easy task. I had done a lot of trading card games, but many of the companies I tried to talk to did not feel that would translate into board game design and initially would not take meetings with me. That changed when John Zinser and AEG gave me a break and published my game *Thunderstone*. After that, most of the publishers were at least willing to talk to me and look at what I was pitching. When *Star Trek Fleet Captains* and *Quar-*

riors came out, I found the companies to be much more receptive. I was also able to convince another company to do another Japanese trading card game, *Battle Spirits*, which ended up being wildly successful as well, and I even ended up with my own anime character in the Battle Spirits TV show. I look like a cross between Elvis and Geordi La Forge.

The moral is, while hard work and pushing yourself will help get you ahead in the game design field, for me I was more often a leaf in the wind, seizing on random opportunities and encounters as they came by. Banging on doors helps a lot, but being lucky and having a few open in front of you never hurts.

TOP DOWN DESIGN
(FEATURING STAR TREK FLEET CAPTAINS)

by Mike Elliott

Over the years I have worked on a lot of IPs. That is Intellectual Properties for anyone who is not in the business. There are two types of design. Spec designs generally start from the bottom up with an interesting play pattern or mechanic, and then a theme is layered on top of the mechanic. Top down designs generally start with an IP and the game is designed around the existing story elements. Top down designs are generally constrained by the world it takes place in. If it is a medieval fantasy world, you can't have motorized airplanes doing strafing runs to take out the orcs at Helms Deep. For these types of games you have to familiarize yourself with the source material and try to represent that in the game. The players expect the game to represent the elements they know and love in the world you are representing.

I used to joke about having an IP Bingo card and that my goal was to fill it. While it started out as a joke, so far I have worked on many of the major properties, including Star Wars, Lord of the Rings, Magic, Harry Potter, Dungeons and Dragons, Simpsons, Pokémon, Halo, Shadowrun, Marvel Comics, DC Comics, Teenage Mutant Ninja Turtles, MechWarrior, Battle Spirits, Yugioh!, Hunger Games, Neopets, Duel Masters, Disney Club Penguin, and Star Trek. People always ask me what my dream IP to work on would be, but I have pretty much covered all of my favorites. Probably the top one I have not worked on and I would like to work on would be Doctor Who.

Star Trek has always been one of my personal favorites. I was a small child when the original series came out, but Star Trek, along with Gilligan's Island, I Love Lucy, and a few others, were the main early syndicated shows. In the 1970s I was living in Phoenix and a local station would show it at 4 PM on weekdays. School got out at 3:40 and I would bike home as quickly as I could to get home before it started, since VCRs were just coming out and my family did not own one. You had to watch it live or wait for it to show again in the episode rotation. At one point, my bike was stolen and for a while I daily ran over 2 miles in the blazing heat to get home to see my favorite show. In fact, one could credit Star Trek for me ending up on the school Cross Country team.

Over the years I watched every episode of the original series (79), Star Trek: The Next Generation (178), Star Trek Deep Space Nine (176), Voyager (172), Enterprise (98), and even the animated series (22). I have also watched every movie, and yes, I do own a pair of Vulcan ears. It would be illogical not to.

The first convention I ever went to was a small science fiction convention in Phoenix as a teenager, and I remember being amazed at seeing all the various toys and merchandise themed around the property. When *Star Fleet Battles* came out, I of course got a copy and played it quite a bit.

Since I had worked for a while at Wizkids when they were still in Seattle, I had kept up contacts with the company. They approached me in 2009 about doing a game themed around Star Trek, and I was excited to finally be able to get a chance to make a game that Star Trek fans would love. It was a big box game and these types of games take many many hours to balance and develop, so I worked with another talented designer, Ethan Pasternack, on the project.

We wanted every game of *Star Trek Fleet Captains* to feel like you were acting out an episode of Star Trek, so instead of just having a straight combat game, we came up with a system where you could control areas, build star bases, and complete science missions in addition to fighting. These aspects are represented by the Science, Combat, and Influence Mission decks and the game is played to a set number of victory points. You can achieve the victory point goal through missions, encounters, and building starbases. You can also play to blow your opponent to smithereens, which is a good strategy if you play the Klingons.

Almost every decision was made to try to give the game the most replay value possible. The randomized board (*Settlers* style) was designed so that the board was never the same each game and so that you could explore as you played as well. The 10 minidecks on each side were designed so that you could take 4 of the 10 and shuffle build them together to form a combat deck. With 5040 combinations possible from the 10 minidecks, there is a lot of variety in the decks you build. Most of them are themed to fit with specific ships or a particular play style. For example, the Captain Kirk deck has a lot of crew members, which can enhance your ships. The Sensor upgrade deck has a lot of stuff to help you complete science style missions.

I mentioned that we wanted to capture everything about the universe. Well, there are often things that don't fit with combat, exploring, or influence. What kind of Star Trek game would it be without Tribbles? So enter the encounter deck. Basically the mechanic is that whenever you move into a square, you have a chance to get an encounter that varies from tile to tile. This lets the game randomly mess with the players in a very flavorful way. It doesn't make the Euro players happy, but they probably were shaken out with the dice combat system anyway, and you can't lose them twice. There are 50 different encounters ranging from your crew being replaced with evil twins to alien ships trading with you. One of my jokes during design was that if it didn't fit anywhere else, it was obviously an encounter. Like most of my jokes, it is only funny if you are a game designer and even for game designers they are not that funny. If I could tell jokes, do you think I would work 18 hours every day making games?

We had to make a few decisions on what to leave out since the universe is so large, but nowadays you are almost obligated to create expansions for a game if it is even remotely successful. So we carved out the Romulans and a lot of the Deep Space Nine material for expansions, and these came out over the next few years. Currently, you can have a 4 player game with players playing Federation, Klingons, Romulans, and Dominion. The newer sets filled in a lot of the gaps for characters. Even though there are 200 cards in the base game, we had to leave out a lot of popular characters just for space reasons. It is hard to boil down over 700 episodes and movies to a single big box game.

The game had a fairly positive response. Tom Vasel, who seems to like a lot of my stuff (*Quarriors*, *Thunderstone*, and *Dice Masters*) picked *Star Trek Fleet Captains* as his top game the year it came out. In fact, I recall Ignacy writing in his previous book about how Tom convinced him to buy it even though he was not a Star Trek fan at all. It has some issues with broken components and since it was a high priced game the expectations in that area were very high, and I certainly would have loved for the ships to have been painted, but the price ruled that out. I had a friend paint mine and later I changed out the ships in one copy for the *Attack Wing* ships, which are the same models but come prepainted. *Star Trek Fleet Captains* remains the top rated Star Trek game on BGG today, and I'm proud of that, but I mainly hope everyone who plays walks away feeling like they've just watched an episode of one of the shows. While I like Star Wars and Lord of the Rings, Star Trek was the first IP I fell in love with, so it has a special place in my heart and I really enjoyed the opportunity to bring it to life in a game.

Ignacy about Paul:

The first time I met Paul was at the Gama Trade Show in Vegas. I was introduced to him by Mike Selinker. Paul said something like: "Nice to meet you, I love your Zombiaki" and in a split second I was like blown away.

You are now probably wondering what the hell is Zombiaki.

I was rather like "How the hell he knows Zombiaki?!"

Zombiaki is my small card game published back in 2003 and printed in a very small print run in English in 2010. How the hell did Paul manage to grab a copy? How did he connect the dots and recognize me as the designer of this small card game?

And the most important – how the hell I was supposed to not love him?

A couple of years ago Portal Games published one of his games - designed with James Ernest - Unexploded Cows. No surprise I published this game in Poland, huh?

And believe me or not, but this game has a very special place – it is in the Top10 best games ever according to my beloved Merry.

Paul designed and co-designed plenty of amazing games with Smash Up and Pathfinder Adventure Card Game being the most famous and I can't wait to have his newest co-design in my hands – Apocrypha. This will be huge.

MY BIGGEST MISTAKE

by Paul Petersen

My first published game was *Guillotine*, in 1998. Why Wizards of the Coast took a chance on a game about cutting off the heads of nobles I may never know, but I'm grateful to this day that they did. I am very proud of the game and truly gratified when I see people playing it today.

In 1998, I had been working in Wizards of the Coast R&D for about 3 years, working on all of the collectible card games from *Magic* to *Vampire* to *Netrunner*. It was an intense environment, full of passionate designers, crazy ideas, and hard work. It's hard to imagine a better crucible for forging a card game designer, and I felt pretty confident in my abilities.

Guillotine came out of a lunch conversation about the French Revolution, where we joked about what it must have been like to be a professional headsman, honing your craft, trying to win awards, and becoming the best headsman anyone had ever seen. After that lunch I kept thinking about that theme and about how to make a game out of it. I've always loved fun, simple card games and I thought this would be great practice to further enhance my skills. I didn't expect it to go anywhere; after all, it was about killing people. But when I built the prototype and got some of the other designers to play it with me, we had a great time. I showed more people, and more people liked it, and before I knew it, there was talk about Wizards publishing it. I was in heaven! And to their credit, the powers that be never once tried to seriously convince me to change the theme.

If you're not familiar with *Guillotine*, the basic mechanic is that there is a line of noble cards. On a player's turn, they can play a card which will usually change the order of the line and then "collect" whatever noble is at the front. At the end of the game, whoever collects the nobles worth the most points wins!

I finished up the design and another designer, Glenn Elliott, took over to go over the design with fresh eyes. Christopher Rush (of *Black Lotus* fame) was the art director, and his vision of the Disney-esque art to offset the theme takes the game to another level. Glenn and I talked a lot about the game, but I remember one conversation in particular about the card Callous Guards.

Callous Guards reads, "Put this card in front of you. Action cards that alter the line may not be played. (This includes adding or discarding nobles.) You may discard this card at any time." *Guillotine* is very chaotic and it can be hard for a player to plan for more than their current turn. This card gives the player a measure of control. They can guarantee which nobles each player will get and can plan their next turns accordingly.

The conversation Glenn and I had was about how long this effect should last. The card I submitted is very close to the one that was printed. Most cards in the game are played, have an effect and are immediately discarded, but Callous Guards sticks around until the player who played it chooses to end the effect on their turn. But it didn't have to be that way. It could have been a normal action that lasted a turn, for example. We were trying to figure out which version we liked best.

We decided to let the card stay in play. There were a lot of good reasons for this. First of all, it lets a player plan their moves out strategically. Secondly, leaving it in play makes it interact more with other cards in the set that specifically target cards on the table. And finally, we assumed that the player wouldn't want to keep it around very long, because they would see better moves on later turns, so it wouldn't be a problem.

I thought we had created one of the most interesting cards in the game. It didn't play like other cards, so it would break up the gameplay in a good way. I thought the other players would enjoy the chance to play the action cards that didn't specifically move nobles in the line. And some of this is true, but is far outweighed by the damage this card does to the game.

Over the years, I've played a lot of *Guillotine* and I've talked to a lot of fans about the game. I noticed a recurring theme in their comments and my experiences. Whenever someone would play Callous Guards, everyone else would suddenly start behaving differently. They'd lose interest in what was going on because they didn't have any more control. They might have something to play that didn't affect the line, but more often than not the only thing they would do on their turn was draw a new card and pass to the next player. They stopped having fun.

The core of *Guillotine* is fun, fast play. It's a light game, which is why many people tell me about how they use it when playing with their "non-gamer" friends. It's full of irreverent humor and simple combos that make the player feel smart. It's not about ruining someone else's plans. The few other "attack" cards in the game do things like swap heads, which increases the chaos and fun; they don't remove it. And that is essentially what Callous Guards does; it removes the core gameplay and turns off everyone's fun except possibly for the person who played it, and often the game isn't even fun for that person. They aren't playing cards either. They're just waiting to see if discarding the card is a good idea. I've even seen that player discard the card when it's better to keep it in play, just because they wanted to play a fun card that changed the line.

Noticing all of this behavior and really thinking about it made me realize what a mistake I had made. It is almost never the right design call to allow players to turn off part of your game, especially not the core gameplay, and never for an extended period of time. Mechanics should always strive to increase the fun for as many players as possible, not just for one of them.

I now look for these interactions when I'm designing a game and question anything that comes close to them. If it's spoiling the experience of most of the players so that one of them can have some control or fun, I generally cut it immediately. After all, games should be fun for everyone.

Vangelis
Bagiartakis

Vangelis Bagiartakis

VANGELIS
GIARTAKIS

VANGELIS BAGIARTAKIS

VANGELIS BAGIARTAKIS

Vangelis
Bagiartakis

VANGELIS BAGIARTAKIS

Ignacy about Vangelis:

This is the moment when we have to ask this question – designers, what's wrong with you? Why do you have such crazy names? Trzewiczek? Chaboussit? Bagiartakis? Really?! Are you kidding me?

Jokes aside. Vangelis is the most famous designer from Greece. He is for Artipia Games - in my humble opinion - like Michał Oracz for Portal Games. A gem. Michał Oracz created amazing Neuroshima Hex for us and bunch of great expansions, Vangelis designed amazing Among the Stars and keeps introducing new expansion for the game on regular basis. As I said - such a designer is a gem.

I did not have enough time to hang out and get to know Vangelis better. Ee met a few times at Essen but it was always in rush, in a hurry, with only a few words and go back to work. My Merry though is constantly talking about visiting Greece and knowing I have friends there like Konstantinos from Artipia Games and Vangelis himself, I am pretty sure I will visit Greece very soon. And my plan is to have some good gaming with this guy!

In the meantime, please, check his new game Dice City and keep an eye on his new projects!

 Follow him on twitter: @vbagiartakis

SO YOU WANT TO BE A GAME DESIGNER?

by Vangelis Bagiartakis

You love board games. You've been playing them with your friends for years. You are having a great time and you keep bringing more people into the hobby. You try all the new releases and you check boardgamegeek on a daily (hourly?) basis.

But that's not enough anymore. You now have ideas of your own. You are thinking of games you played and changes that could be applied to make them even better. You have thought of a cool combination of mechanics that nobody has used before and you are sure it is going to be the next best thing!

You are also thinking about the current board gaming scene: Look at all those new designers who have their game published! Look at all those successful Kickstarter projects! Look at all those conventions, how happy the designers are, seeing their games played by gamers from all over the world! Since they made it, why not you? Your idea is definitely better than theirs, and you can easily prove it!

So you want to be a game designer, huh?

That's great! But you need to know what you are getting into. No, I don't mean getting to learn the theory behind game design, things like game flow, player experience, iteration processes, and interest curves. You've probably read about them already in other books and articles.

I'm talking about the real thing. What it *really* means to be a game designer. What (probably) nobody else is going to tell you...

(well, perhaps nobody except Ignacy)

So you want to be a game designer?

Do you have a family? Wife and kids perhaps? Oh, they are going to love your new endeavor! Let me give you some real-life examples:

July, 2012

We are on vacation. My wife, my 2 year old son, my baby daughter and I are visiting my parents-in-law's summer house for a few days. Try to imagine the scene: The sun is shining, the beach is nearby, the grandparents are playing with the kids, my wife is resting, reading a novel and I... I am in front of a computer checking some files. *Among the Stars* is about to be sent to the printers and I need to approve the files as soon as possible. So I'm going through the PDFs with the cards, the rulebook, the punchboards, the box art, and so on and so on.

I send a list of corrections. The next day I receive the updated files from the graphic designer. The sun is still shining, the beach is still gleaming, and the rest of the family is still spending time with the kids. I am going through the files once again, very thoroughly, to make sure all the corrections have been applied correctly. I notice a few things I hadn't spotted before and I send a new list.

The next day is more or less the same. Sun, beach, kids, and me working. A few adjustments in the text of some of the abilities need to be made to maintain consistency throughout the game. Some clarifications are made in the manual, pdf files and notes keep coming and going, and Skype is chockfull of heated discussions.

What's more, during these days, while I am not checking files, I'm constantly on the phone with some of the playtesters. The crowdfunding campaign for the game that ended a few days earlier has generated some promos that are being tested. "What about this card?", "Hmm, perhaps we need to lower its cost after all", "What if we change this in the effect?" and so on. The phone is on fire. The cards' abilities need to be finalized in order to have the graphic designer prepare them and send the files to me. I need to thoroughly check them, send a list of corrections, get the new files, check them again, send corrections, and so on and so on...

This goes on for days. At some point my wife gives me the look. THAT look. "You know we are on vacation, right?" She is not very happy with how our vacation is turning out.

The files, however, need to be sent to the printers and time is of the essence...

July, 2013

One year has passed. Once again we are on vacation, but this time, *Among the Stars: The Ambassadors* is being prepared for release in Essen. As luck will have it, the schedule of the artist, the graphic designer and the publisher is such that the deadline for the files have ended up once again right in the middle of my vacation.

Yes, the universe sometimes really likes to mess with you.

I won't bother you with the details - just go back and reread the previous year's story. Copy. Paste.

And yes, once again I got THAT look from my wife...

January 2, 2015

This time it's winter vacation. We have arranged with some friends to take our families and go away for a few days. Heavy snow makes for a great new year's eve, but I end up catching a cold the day after. On January 2nd we go sight-seeing in the nearby areas. Not feeling very well, I let my wife drive. After a while I get a phone call.

It's a publisher with whom I have been working for the last month. I am developing a game he is planning to take with him to Nuremberg, and time is REALLY pressing us. I had sent all the necessary emails before leaving, but there are questions, and a few clarifications are needed. We are going over the cards and I'm explaining some of the changes. All this while I'm in the car, with my wife at the wheel, my kids in the back, and a terrible headache...

So you want to be a game designer?

Do you like staying up late? Like, really late? Your answer had better be yes because it comes with the territory.

April, 2015

I am taking part in a board game competition. Along with a friend of mine we have designed a historical wargame and on Sunday an event is scheduled in which all the competition's participants can show off their games to the public, have them playtested and get valuable feedback. It is not the final day of the competition, but it is super important for us.

The game is the heaviest game I have worked on so far. The whole week I am in constant discussions with my co-designer about it, changing things, getting rid of cards, adding new effects, and so on. The cards keep changing, but sometime late on Friday the spreadsheet in which we keep the cards is more or less finalized (for the moment), and we have agreed on some changes that need to be made to the board.

Saturday comes. It's a super busy day with all kinds of family matters. At some point around 9 pm I am finally able to work on the prototype. The cards' abilities may have been "finalized", but they still need to be turned into actual physical cards. The same goes for the board. There are many changes since the last printed version, so we definitely need to print a new one.

I start with the board. After a couple of hours of copying, cutting, pasting, cropping, moving, and filling it is mostly done. It's around midnight and I start on the cards. One hour later I am still working on the cards. By now I have some questions for my co-designer, but it is too late to call. Another hour later I am still working on the cards. Since they are (hopefully) going to be seen by many people, I want them to look the best they can. It's not just a playtesting session with friends where you could, for example, get away with hand-written cards. This is important. I want them to look attractive so that a random passer-by will want to sit down and try the game. But this means extra work. Another hour passes.

And another.

Around 4:30 a.m. I am finished with the digital files and I start printing. I can't keep my eyes open, but I need to assemble the board out of the separate sheets printed, cut the cards, and put them in sleeves. I am too sleepy to do everything - I cut the board and some of the cards and leave the rest for the next day.

I go to sleep a little after 5, having to wake up about three hours later...

The event starts and for the first 20 minutes or so, my co-designer and I are cutting cards and putting them in sleeves. After a while we are finally ready and I have to admit, the game looks quite nice.

Strangely enough, I manage not to fall asleep at the table during the event.

So you want to be a game designer?

Are you good with math? Do you have experience with spreadsheets? How familiar are you with formulas and algorithms? If you're not, then better find someone who is!

You see, behind almost every game out there, there lies a mathematical model. This action is worth that much, the power level of this card is that high, this resource is twice as valuable as that one, and so on. Even if a designer did it empirically, without actually calculating the values but using many playtests as his guide, a model is there.

When the time comes to balance a game you make, being aware of its model (and using it) is going to make your life significantly easier. But this comes at a price. Depending on the game, you may end up spending a lot of time in front of a computer screen. Let me share with you a personal story...

May-June, 2015

I am doing development work on a game. The game is great fun, it has a very nice theme, and it does a great job at conveying it to the players. It's quite easy to play, but there is a small "problem" as far as development is concerned. It has lots and lots of cards, with lots and lots of values on them. Balancing it is a killer.

I analyze the math behind it, I assign values to resources, I calculate some formulas and I start working on each card. Cell by cell, card by card, sheet by sheet I move on. I check if they are balanced, I apply changes where necessary, I adjust things if needed and I move on. And on and on and on...

But they just don't end.

I end up spending not minutes, not hours, but days on these cards. All this time while staring at my computer screen.

My eyes hurt and my mind is probably fried. But now that I am finished with the spreadsheet I need to "create" these cards digitally so that I can then print a prototype.

I know there are ways to take a spreadsheet file and automatically create cards out of it, but the nature of this game is such that you can't do that effectively. It has to be done manually for every card.

Did I mention that there are a lot of cards?

It ends up taking almost double the time the balancing took. After a few days I am done. I get the files printed and we sit down to play some games. A few games are enough to give us a good idea: this resource is not that valuable, that one is more important than we thought, that action should change, and the formula on this type of cards needs to be adjusted. The changes may sound small, but in reality they affect the vast majority of the cards in a significant way.

I repeat the whole process again, once more spending countless hours in front of my pc. If my brain was fried before, now it has actually melted.

I print the cards again and we play. The changes are definitely an improvement. The game flows much better, more things make sense, but a few playtests in we realize another problem that was not apparent before. We discuss how to deal with this and we end up slightly changing the way a type of card works. From a player's point of view it is not that big of a change. You only need to change 1 or 2 sentences in the rules. As far as development is concerned, however... - you guessed it - the whole sheet with these cards needs to be remade.

As I am writing these lines I have finished the third major pass on this game's cards. Let's hope the changes from now on are on a much smaller scale...

So you want to be a game designer?

How many times do you usually play a game before getting bored with it? 5? 10? 20? 50? Get ready to put these numbers to shame. After all, there is a reason they call game design an **iterative** process.

They say that if you haven't gotten sick of your game, then you probably haven't playtested it enough. Even if you reach that point, you may still need to play twice the number of games you've already played. After all, the amount of playtesting is what often separates a good game from a great one.

Of course, there is a reason why this is the case. The more times you play it, the more different situations will come up, and if there are problems in the game, you will have that many more chances to catch them. Here's another relevant story...

March 2015

A game I have been working on for months is about to be sent to the printers. At that point I have played it about 70-80 (documented) times and a few more that I never bothered to write down. Everything has been more or less finalized and I am just doing some final playtests to make sure one of the last things we changed, works okay. The game is simple to play and has no hidden information, so it is very easy for me to play quick "2-player games" on my own to test things. This has the added bonus of getting to put 2 "players" with the exact same experience and skill against each other (me and... myself!), allowing for any misbalance in different strategies to become apparent more easily.

At some point, after a few games, I begin to suspect something. It doesn't have to do with that last change I was testing for, but with something more inherent in the game. Now that I am aware of it, I start playing around it and it soon becomes obvious.

One of the strategies is broken.

If you follow a series of very specific steps, almost regardless of what cards come up or what you roll, you end the game (victorious) before the other player has a chance to do so. Three or four games in a row prove the theory beyond a doubt. I share my findings with another person who has also played the game many times, and he is very skeptical at first. We sit down and play. He doesn't know what hits him...

The good thing was that I caught this before the game was sent to the printers. The bad thing was that I had to immediately find a solution that would not change the game significantly, leading to other potential problems down the road.

Luckily for me, having played the game so many times gave me a very good understanding of how everything worked on the inside. This in turn helped me analyze the problem and identify what exactly was causing it: it wasn't in the game's cards or in any of its main mechanisms. The game breaking strategy was just triggering one of the end game conditions too soon. Adjusting just that trigger with a very subtle change would be enough to fix the problem and bring balance to the forc.. ehm, the game.

If I hadn't played the game as many times as I had, I wouldn't have found the problem. More than a 100 games had been played (other people were also testing it, not only me) without it rearing its ugly head.

Are you prepared to play your game more than 100 times to make sure it is ready for publication?

So you want to be a game designer?

Congratulations, it is one of the best decisions you've ever made. But as you can see, game design is not an easy task. However, we do it with all our heart. Not because of the money it will bring us or the fame, but because we love it. We truly, truly love it.

This is what drives us. This is what gives us passion, inspiration, and strength to overcome any obstacles. This is what keeps us awake at night working on a game, allows us to play the same game again and again even though we are sick of it, gets us to sacrifice our free time. We love what we do, every second of it.

We wouldn't have it any other way.

Stephen King, in the introduction to one of his books, said something very important about writing:

"...you don't do it for money, or you're a monkey. You don't think of the bottom line, or you're a monkey. You don't think of it in terms of hourly wage, yearly wage, even lifetime wage, or you're a monkey. In the end you don't even do it for love, although it would be nice to think so. You do it because to not do it is suicide."

It's the same with game design.

Stephen Buonocore

STEPHEN BUONOCORE

STEPHEN BUONOCORE

Stephen Buonocore

Stephen Buonocore

STEPHEN BUONOCORE

Ignacy about Anythony:

One of the most distinctive people in the industry. Stephen Buonacore himself.

Known as the Podfather because he is a guest on every single podcast there is. You might invite him, you might not invite him, it doesn't matter, he will be a guest on your show. Period.

Known as the nemesis of Tom Vasel, because for years they pretend to hate each other and trash talk each time they meet.

Known as the life and soul of the party on every convention he attends. Because of Black PR campaign on my humble persona lately also known as The Only Host of Board Games Insider Who Knows How To Party.

(You can throw a pretty awesome drinking tea party!!!)

He is funny, passionate, and kind. He helped me a lot, and I hope I will be able to help him too someday.

And because this is a fragment about Stephen, we need to have a sales pitch, huh? Buy Stronghold, 2nd edition. Now! :)

 Follow him on twitter: @strongholdgames

IGNACY TRZEWICZEK

WHY I LOVE TOM VASEL

An Essay of Love by Stephen M. Buonocore

How do I love thee, Tom Vasel? Let me count the ways...

Okay, let's not get crazy here. I really do love Tom Vasel, and likely I can count the ways. However, as poetry is not my strong suit, and my love for Tom is bro-mantic, not romantic, I would rather take you on a little trip down my very own "Tom Vasel Memory Lane". This Memory Lane is not a very long road, but it does pre-date Stronghold Games.

My first communication with Tom Vasel was via email in 2007. Stronghold Games, which was founded in late 2009, was not yet a glimmer in my eye. Just like you, I was an ordinary listener of The Dice Tower, and I participated in one of the contests that Tom and then co-host Sam Healy ran on the show... and I won!

To claim my prize, I emailed Tom, and in my salutation and signature, I wrote the following:

Best,

Stephen "The Evil One"

p.s. "The Evil One" is a gaming nickname. I'm not really evil (and in fact I'm really good and nice), so don't worry... :) :)

Tom refers back to this moment, noting to me "You called yourself *evil* from the start!"

I believe that it was because of this moniker that Tom has attempted to smite me ever since.

I continued to write to him at various times that year, once saying to him:

> *The Dice Tower is "The Variety Show" of game podcasts...This is what I love about your show. Some criticize this, but I love it, and you should embrace this. It really works for you. Keep adding more segments and features, and people will continue to flock to you.*
>
> *Your show is the best of the podcasts, so keep up the great work!"*

As you can see, my love of Tom Vasel started way back in 2007.

In 2010, Stronghold Games released its first game, *Code 777*. Realizing the publicity power of the podcast, I attempted to get on The Dice Tower. Tom would not have this. I dealt with my rejection by turning to my buddy Geoff Engelstein, who of course even back then had the *"Game Tek"* segment on The Dice Tower. I made Geoff an offer he could not refuse, and he interviewed me for his segment, which aired in episode #176 of The Dice Tower.

I believe Tom's reaction to this momentous event in Dice Tower history was *"Hmmm...very sneaky."*

Back in 2010, there weren't dozens of noted reviewers in the industry, there was just Tom Vasel. As a new company with a new game, having Tom review the game was of paramount importance to me. So, I wrote to Tom and asked:

Would you be able to do a review of "Code 777" in the near future? Preferably, it would be great to have you do it before the end of July, or very early August, as our preorder window closes on/about August 11 (when the bulk of the games hits the US shores), but I will take what I can get. Even if you review it later, I know you will do a great job and help push retail sales as well..."

I believe Tom's reaction to my request was *"Hmmm...and he's pushy..."*

Tom and I finally met face to face at Origins 2011. Hearing that Tom was going to have a Dice Tower booth at the show, I reached out and asked if he would like to cooperate on booth space, co-locating the booths and generally helping each other out. Amazingly, to this Tom said *"Let's do this!"*

Stronghold Games had its first 3 releases at Origins 2011, *Code 777*, *Confusion*, and *Survive: Escape From Atlantis!*. I was so happy to be working with Tom! As soon as we were all setup and ready for the show, Tom looked over my games… and nodded approvingly!

Tom then said, *"So when are you going to release a bad game?"*

I just replied, *"Ummm... Thank you, Tom."*

Later that year, I convinced Tom to actually let me on The Dice Tower, as I gave him a huge scoop on an impending game release. On The Dice Tower show, I gave Tom, Eric Summerer, and the world this huge news… Stronghold Games would be re-printing *Merchant of Venus!*

And then just a few month later, I appeared again on The Dice Tower, this time bringing with me my now good friend Christian T. Peterson, President of Fantasy Flight Games, to re-announce that Fantasy Flight Games would be re-printing *Merchant of Venus*.

Oh yeah… Those were good times back then…

Tom and I have gone to many dinners together over the years. Tom really likes to eat. Really really. So, when Tom and I find ourselves in the same place, a dinner is almost always on the schedule. At Gen Con 2013, Tom, Eric, Zee Garcia, Chad Mekash and myself found ourselves in search of a dining establishment. Walking up Maryland

Street from the Convention Center, Eric said, *"This place looks fun."* The restaurant was *Dick's Last Resort.*

You need to fathom the irony of Pastor Tom Vasel being in a restaurant like *Dick's Last Resort.* The wait staff is purposefully mean to you. They yell at you, they won't tell you what they will bring you, they belittle you, and they make you wear stupid hats. Of course, it is all in good fun, but the place is crazy. But it just starts there. Here are some of the slogans on the souvenir T-shirts that you can buy at this place:

Chicks Love Dick's

They Have Hooters, We Have Dick's

I Like It Dirty

Dick U (as in "University"...ahem)

Tom sits down in *Dick's Last Resort,* looks around, and immediately says *"I'm not sure I can eat here."*

Two hours later, after wearing the silly paper hats, getting chewed out by the waitress, and laughing our butts off, Tom tells Eric, *"You are never picking the restaurant again."*

Tom badgered me for years to come to Dice Tower Con. I would have loved to have gone from the beginning, but due to other commitments including a local New Jersey convention that is at the same time as Dice Tower Con each year, I have not been able to go. However, in 2015, there was no scheduling conflict, so I went as a guest of Tom Vasel to Dice Tower Con.

Tom took me to the Polynesian at Disney for dinner at Dice Tower Con. This dinner was for the biggest Dice Tower Kickstarter backers, and Tom invited me as a Guest of Honor, which was very nice of him. We were both in rare form, mocking each other incessantly for the comedic benefit of the backers. Our waitress was amazing, so very Disney-friendly and animated. I went into "Buonocore Charming Mode", and started flirting with the waitress. Without hesitation, Tom whips out his phone, and within seconds, shows the waitress a picture of my girlfriend. Tom performs a *"Buonocore Block"* for the win!

I have become known as The *Podfather* due to my Italian heritage and my penchant for appearing on every board gaming podcast possible. However, appearing on everyone else's podcast was not enough. The Podfather needed to have access to the millions of board game podcast listeners out there on a more regular basis. Ignacy Trzewiczek invited me to start a podcast with him called *"Board Games Insider"*. When I told Tom that Ignacy and I had started this podcast, and that we were bringing a fresh, new, concise, bi-weekly, 30-minute look at the hobby game industry, Tom said to me, *"You won't make it to 10 episodes."*

After episode 10 of *Board Games Insider*, it was an honor that Tom Vasel invited us onto The Dice Tower Network. Secretly, I think Tom really loves me back.

And honestly, we really do love each other. We have a great friendship and a mutual admiration for what the other does and has accomplished. Truly, Tom is one of the most genuine, nice, friendly, intelligent, and loving people that you will ever meet. It is an honor for me to call Tom Vasel my friend.

When Geoff Engelstein heard that I was writing an article entitled *"Why I Love Tom Vasel"*, his tweeted comment was *"This will be the shortest chapter ever."*

I love proving a genius wrong. Sorry, Geoff. I really do love Tom Vasel.

Stephen M. Buonocore
President, Stronghold Games LLC
Arch Nemesis of Tom Vasel

Merry
Trzewiczek

Merry Trzewiczek

MERRY
TRZEWICZEK

Merry
Trzewiczek

MERRY
TRZEWICZEK

MADNESS

by Merry Trzewiczek

Autumn is coming. Not Winter. The Autumn. It's gold, sunny, and a bit rainy. And smells nice. I love Autumn. For me it has the smell of wet leaves, fog, rain and... new games. For many years Autumn means Essen.

Every Essen is a big adventure. With Ignacy, every Essen is a big adventure. Another adventure with my husband. I am not a very romantic person. When I think about my husband I know I have very strong feelings for him though.

I think I love him. But why?

Maybe because he can cook?
No. He can't. He hardly ever cooks.

Maybe because he can sing?
No! He can't.

Maybe because he is very romantic?
He is as romantic as my pendrive.

Maybe because he loves animals?
Yes. On his plate.

Maybe because he can spend a night talking with me?
Hm… if night lasts ten minutes…

Maybe because he is handsome.
Come on! Jeff Goldblum is handsome! Bob Geldof is handsome!

Maybe because he wakes up every morning in a good mood.
If the morning starts at noon… before 8 a.m. he doesn't even have „a mood".

Maybe because he loves the same books as me?
If the same means ‚made of paper'.

Maybe because he likes the same movies as me?
If the same means ‚with actors'.

Maybe because he loves the mountains like me?
Yes, if the mountains surround a board games convention.

Maybe because he likes the sea like me?
Yes, if it is the only way to go to a board games convention.

Maybe because we like the same food?
Yes, if the same means „tomatoes".

Maybe because we love the same sports?
„MerryThisWasAmazingGoalYouHaveToWatchIt!!!" No.

Maybe because we have the same friends?
No! In his world people who don't like board games simply don't exist.

Maybe because we like the same games?
Yes. Two or three…

Maybe because I am the biggest fan of his games?!
I am not.

Maybe because he can make me furious in one second?
Oh yes! Don't ask me why.

Maybe because he can makes me laugh every day? Even if he doesn't want to me to laugh at him?
Yes! Very yes!

And finally the thing I do love most is his IQ. Being with him, I know I will never become a ‚stupid woman'. Because I have no chance. Because I can't. Because every day I have to exercise my mind to react to his stupid jokes!

boardgames
that tell
stories.com

boardgames that
tell stories.com

BOARDGAMES
THAT TELL
STORIES.COM

FOLLOW ME!

HTTP://BOARDGAMESTHATTELLSTORIES.COM @trzewik

BOARDGAMES THAT TELL STORIES 2

FIRST EDITION

Designed by Maciej Mutwil
(based on Rafał Szyma project)
Editor: Michiel Hendriks

ISBN: 9788360525500

Portal Games
Św. Urbana 15 St.
44-100 Gliwice
Poland

http://portalgames.pl
portal@portalgames.pl
tel. +48 32 334 8538